STARGAZING

STARGAZING

Memoirs of a Young Lighthouse Keeper

Peter Hill

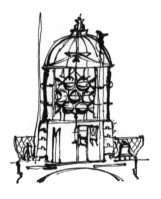

McArthur
&
Company
Toronto

For permission to reprint, acknowledgment is made to the following:

Excerpt from 'I Feel Like I'm Fixin' To Die Rag', words and music by Joe McDonald © 1965 Alkatraz Corner Music Co. Used by permission; Lines from 'Flannan Isle' from Collected Poems by W.W. Gibson, copyright by The Estate of W.W. Gibson. Reprinted by permission of the publisher, Macmillan, London, UK; Lines from The Collected Poems of Langston Hughes by Langston Hughes, copyright ©1994 by The Estate of Langston Hughes. Used by permission of Alfred A. Knopf, a division of Random House, Inc; Lines by Flann O'Brien from The Third Policeman by Flann O'Brien. Copyright © 1967 Evelyn O'Nolan; 'Strange Days' Words and Music by The Doors Copyright © 1967 Doors Music Co. Copyright Renewed All Rights Reserved. Used by Permission; From 'Venus in Furs' by the Velvet Underground, words copyright © Lou Reed, permission approved by EMI Music Publishing; From 'Flowers in the Rain' by The Move, copyright © 1967 Westminster Music Limited of Suite 207, Plaza 535 Kings Road, London SW10 0SZ, international copyright secured, used by permission; From the poetry of Hermann Hesse, copyright © The Estate of Herman Hesse, permission granted from Suhrkamp Verlag (Germany); From 'On John MacLean' from the collection The New Divan by Edwin Morgan, reprinted by permission of the publisher, Carcanet Press Ltd; From 'Vindaloo in Merthyr Tydfil' in Learning Human: New Selected Poems, 2001, by Les Murray, reproduced by permission of the publisher, Duffy and Snellgrove (Australia and New Zealand), reproduced by permission of the publisher, Carcanet (UK/ Commonwealth excluding Australia and New Zealand), reproduced by permission of the publisher Farrar, Straus and Giroux, New York; From the poetry of John Arden, reprinted by permission of the author; From 'The Heart of the Matter' by Graham Greene, copyright © The Estate of Graham Greene, reprinted by permission of the publisher, Random House; From 'Bagpipe Music' by Louis MacNiece, reproduced by permission of the publisher, Faber.

First published in Canada in 2004 by
McArthur & Company
322 King St. West, Suite 402
Toronto, Ontario, M5V 1J2
www.mcarthur-co.com
10 9 8 7 6 5 4 3 2 1

National Library of Canada Cataloguing in Publication

Hill, Peter, 1953-
  Stargazing : memoirs of a young lighthouse keeper / Peter Hill.

ISBN 1-55278-411-8

  1. Hill, Peter, 1953- 2. Nineteen seventies. 3. Social values.
  4. Lighthouse keepers--Biography. I. Title.
VK1140.H54A3 2004   387.1'55'092   C2003-907466-8

Illustrations by David Faithfull
Typeset by Palimpsest Book Production Ltd., Creative Print & Design, Ebbw Vale, Wales
Printed in Canada by Friesens

This book is dedicated to:
'The Last Lighthouse Keeper' – wherever you are.
Shine on Brightly . . .

. . . and to my wife Sally,
both our families, and all our two-legged
and four-legged friends

Anythin' for a quiet life, as the man said
when he took the sitivation at the lighthouse.
Charles Dickens 1812–70: *The Pickwick Papers* (1837)

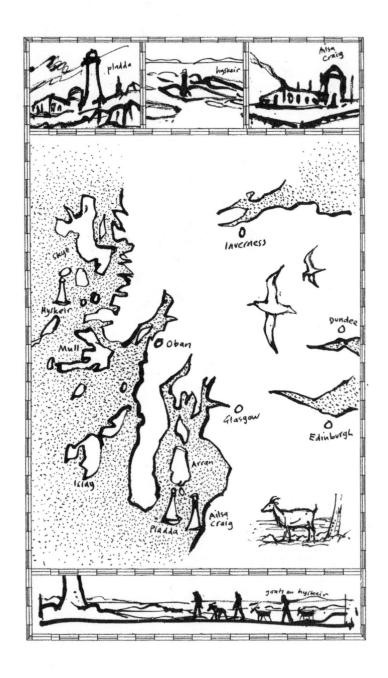

Contents

Part Three – Ailsa Craig

Part Four – Hyskeir

Postscript

Introduction

Ahoy!

In 1973 I worked as a lighthouse keeper on three islands off the west coast of Scotland. Before taking the job I didn't really think through what a lighthouse keeper actually did. I was attracted by the romantic notion of sitting on a rock, writing haikus and dashing off the occasional watercolour. The light itself didn't seem important: it might have been some weird coastal decoration, like candles on a Christmas tree, intended to bring cheer to those living in the more remote parts of the country.

I was nineteen when I was interviewed for the job of relief keeper by the commissioners of the Northern Lights in the New Town of Edinburgh. My hair hung well below my shoulders. I had a great set of Captain Beefheart records and I walked about with a permanent grin on my face as I had recently, finally, lost my virginity. I rolled my own cigarettes, was a member of Amnesty International and had just read Kerouac's *Desolation Angels*. In short, I was eminently suitable for the job.

HOW I LANDED
THE JOB

The Tavern Bar

'How on earth did you get a job as a lighthouse keeper?' In the thirty-odd years since landing the job that's been the most frequently asked question in the different parts of the world that I've lived and travelled. I've been asked by taxi drivers in Hong Kong, Tasmania, and Chicago, and at dinner parties in Paris and Sydney. 'And what exactly do you *do* in a lighthouse?' is, nine times out of ten, the follow-up question.

To answer the first question I take my interrogators back to the Tavern Bar in Dundee, a bar so wonderful that in my thoughts it is up there with the Admiral Benbow in Stevenson's *Treasure Island*. In the early Seventies it was frequented by as motley a bunch of patrons as you could hope to find. Think of the inter-galactic bar in *Star Wars*, then add a bit of Marx Brothers slapstick, and if you know Chick Murray the genius many consider Scotland's greatest comedian, then there's more than a bit of him in there too. Bars are wonderful places for adventures to begin . . .

The back room of the Tavern Bar in Dundee was where we used to play darts as young art students. The Tav was an art school institution and, like Scotland herself, has a long history. The nine-teenth-century poet William McGonagall used to frequent it and read his magnificently dreadful poems for a few pennies in the very back room where we honed our darts-playing skills in games with bizarre names such as 301, Mickey Mouse and Round-the-Clock. Bert, the landlord, was an avuncular host who kept good order in the house and administered a series of bans on those who overstepped the mark. Some might be banned for a month (the date of re-entry circled on the calendar in his pocket diary), some for only a few nights, and occasionally Bert, with all the compassion of a hanging judge, would bar someone for life.

My time in Dundee during the early Seventies was that rare part of the twentieth century when there was no unemployment. As art students, with a sartorial elegance that predated but rivalled the Muppets, we quaffed ale next to builders, bakers, prostitutes, merchant seamen, inspectors of meat pies, oil rig workers, microwave oven salesmen, white-skinned ex cons re-navigating their lives, and a gang of soft-drug dealers wearing bandannas who looked like they had recently been employed as extras in *The Good, the Bad and the Ugly*. They were in fact town planning students to a man and barely old enough to vote. The legacy of their stoned student days is now cast in concrete in spiralling ring roads that meander around our cities, from Birmingham to Inverness, often leading absolutely nowhere but obviously enjoying travelling hopefully.

The music in our teenage heads was implanted by Radio One, or more exotically Radio Luxembourg, the best-known of the pirate radio stations. I never could find it on the dial and settled for John Peel instead. But his offerings were too gloriously esoteric to define the age – Ivor Cutler, The Third Ear Band, Leonard Cohen (am I the only one who used to think he had a great voice and his songs were actually quite cheerful?), Dave Van

Ronk, Edger Broughton, and The Thirteenth-Floor Elevators. No, the music of the streets was pure Radio One via Tony Blackburn, Dave Lee Travis, and Simon Dee – The Kinks, Dusty Springfield, The Monkees and Sonny and Cher. They guided us through the late sixties and through puberty with the pastoral care of a dentist in a sweet shop – not offering us too much of anything that might start any serious rot. The Beatles were always fine, The Stones a bit dangerous, The Doors . . . well, you had to wait until nightfall, and I think only late on a Wednesday night, for John Peel to appear and The Doors to open. They in turn gave on to a landscape peopled by Grace Slick, The Incredible String Band and The Grateful Dead. Safe and secure in my middle class suburb of Glasgow I would lie beneath the sheets, my homework completed, and listen to Country Joe MacDonald rage against the war in Vietnam, 'Give me an Eff!' he would cry, 'Give me a U! Give me a C! . . . Give me a K! . . . What's that spell?! . . . What's that spell?!' And then he would push out his song, like an angry boat, into the world:

> 'Come on all you big strong men,
> Uncle Sam needs your help again.
> He's got himself in a terrible jam,
> Way down yonder in Vietnam . . .'

And so I would drop off to sleep in a purple haze of adolescent plans for the future. THE FUTURE, a mythical and by definition futuristic place which all my life has been just out there, occasionally signposted, but like algebra or German grammar, never quite graspable. Like that destination board on Ken Kesey's bus that read FUURTHER, never quite within reach . . .

*   *   *

Everyone had plans in those days and the Tav was where they were most often discussed. They were of course based on a full-employment economy. Don't try this at home if you were born any time after 1970. Recently qualified teachers could quit their jobs and hitch to India assured that they would pick up another teaching job, possibly with a promotion, as soon as they returned. A sculptor subsidising their art by working in the parks department could, on a whim, leave for Shetland and find work gutting fish or working for the post office. Others played in rock bands or were fiddle-scraping folk musicians in Aran jumpers and flared jeans. Society was deliciously flexible in those days and all things seemed possible. Carefree pretty much sums it up. Stress had not yet been invented and wouldn't catch on in Scotland until well into the Eighties. But back in the late Sixties and early Seventies you wouldn't see someone for a few months and then suddenly a postcard from a mate would arrive addressed c/o Bert, The Tavern Bar, Dundee, from Venice Beach in California or the Melkweg Club in Amsterdam. In those days the post office took a rather perverse pride in delivering every single piece of mail no matter how scantily it was addressed. Sometimes simply 'Bert, the Tav', would find its destination – very like Banjo Paterson's famous Australian ballad which features a letter addressed to 'Clancy of The Overflow'.

A few friends left for London, like Clancy leaving for the Australian tropics. It was the tail end of the Swinging Sixties, a decade which I like to think started with the Beatles first number-one hit *Love Me Do* in 1962, and ended with the oil crisis in 1974.

Friday night was the big night at the Tav and you had to get there early or else you had to queue, especially if there was to be a band playing in the art school later in the evening. And we got some great bands. Pink Floyd played the art school, as did the legendary Viv Stanshall and The Bonzo Dog Doo Dah Band. The annual Dundee art school Christmas "Revels" were so wild that one passing group called Pete Brown and Piblokta even named their next album in honour of playing there. It was called "*Things May Come and Things May Go But the Art School Dance Goes on Forever,*" and the following term we all rushed out to spend our grant cheques on it.

I remember one 'Revels' that had a Wild West theme and a whole cowboy village was built in the art school hall. I went as a Mexican which befitted my waist length hair and short stature, and I attained a certain verisimilitude by dyeing my skin yellow with textile dye smuggled out of Willie Watt's textile class that afternoon. It was a strange Christmas the following week in Glasgow, as I remember it, surrounded by close family and maiden aunts, me glowing like a beacon at a zebra crossing and feigning jaundice.

Outside the Tav on a Friday it wasn't unusual to see upwards of thirty people queuing in the dark rain by eight in the evening. Once inside, mushroom damp, there was a sunburst of light and a symphony of artistic banter as one ran the gauntlet of three hundred elbows towards the bar for two pints of heavy (one to gulp down quickly, the other to enjoy at one's leisure) and then into the deeply nicotine-stained back room where if you were lucky you could squeeze on to the end of one of the many old school desks with folding chairs that was the sole furniture lining the walls. This was also the nesting place of the serious domino players (or 'bones' players as they were known), and it wasn't unheard of for someone to make as much as ten pounds from a good night in the back room. As often as not, on a Friday, the art school band Mort Wriggle and the Panthers would be playing at the far end of the room, Jonathan 'Jogg' Ogilvie thrashing away on drums. Years later I discovered Jogg was working in a museum in Arbroath while his friend Phil, who dropped out of art school after second year, made it big in London as a rock musician in a band called Camel. After that he re-surfaced in the Eighties as Jessie Rae, king of tartan video rock dressed in a kilt and brandishing a two-handed sword.

In the Tav a pound note would buy eight pints of beer at the newly decimalised price of twelve pence a pint, and there would still be enough change for a packet of Rizla cigarette papers and a box of matches. Whole streets close to the Tav were colonised by art students, but none more so than Kincardine Street. During the week many would return there after ten o'clock closing time to begin 'all-nighters', working till dawn to get assignments finished (good training for an aspiring lighthouse keeper) with perhaps a break at three in the morning to buy a meat pie or a honey dumpling amongst the taxi drivers and ladies of the night at Cuthbert's, the all-night bakers. I never met Mr Cuthbert but can vouch that he did make exceedingly good dumplings.

Recharged, we would talk passionately above the sounds of Frank Zappa, Procol Harum and Jefferson Airplane, of Braque and Picasso and the alpine feats of Analytical Cubism as if Montmartre, rather than Arbroath, was just up the road. The more informed art students would talk of David Hockney and Andy Warhol and how they were giving the lie to the old myth that 'no one will ever take you seriously in the art world until you are over forty'. It was this myth more than anything that allowed art students to take a very long view of life and plan several interesting and varied careers before they finally 'made it' sometime in their early fifties.

The Tav was a different place of a weekday lunchtime. Mostly art students, their lecturers, a few travelling salesmen and the usual gaggle of half-stoned town-planning students building futuristic ring roads with damp beer mats and Swan Vesta matchboxes. The bar always seemed to be filled with light around midday. Going through the western style swing doors was like suddenly entering a cathedral in mid summer. White light, white heat and the gossamer-thin cigarette smoke slowly spiralling upwards. Don Mclean had a song out about that time with a chorus of 'Bye, Bye Miss American Pie' which we altered slightly to 'My, My Miss Dundonian Peh', and that long *eh* – rhyming with Yeah! as in the Beatles 'She Loves You, Yeah! Yeah! Yeah! – Peh! Peh! Peh!' was the hallmark of the Dundee accent then as it is now, 'A peh an' a pint' being as near to heaven as lunch gets by the side of the Silvery Tay, or anywhere else for that matter.

When I was eventually asked to leave the art school I think it was the Tav, and its camaraderie, that I missed most of all. Certainly more so than the brutalist architecture of the art school. This is how my demise happened, and to describe it I have to describe my early beginnings.

I grew up in Glasgow in the early Fifties, born on the fifth of June 1953 – a slow news day shortly after the Queen's Coronation and the conquest of Everest. Throughout childhood everything seemed either black or grey until winter came and things briefly turned white – an exaggeration, of course, but for much of the year colour didn't seem to exist at all. Glasgow's buildings were black with soot from the industrial revolution, so uniformly black that most of my childhood I unquestioningly accepted that this was the natural colour of stone. Some tenements stood like jagged black teeth courtesy of the German war-time bombing of the Clyde, and one of my earliest visual thrills was viewing the patchwork of wallpaper and mantelpieces exposed to the elements down whole sides of opened tenement walls. It looked as good as any installation art I have ever seen, and perhaps it was no coincidence that Joseph Beuys was in the *luftwaffe* at the time.

Television was black and white, text in books was black on white, crossword puzzles, dominoes, Buster Keaton movies, and all the images from the past, from history, came down to me in grainy death camp black and white or nineteenth-century etchings illustrating Dickens, *The Hound of the Baskervilles*, or scenes from the Crimean War. I wanted colour. I absolutely longed for colour. And in my naivety I think deep inside me I just accepted that colour had only come in to the world with the invention of colour photography. So I actively searched for colour. I found it in tubes of paint. Liquid colour, screw off the cap and there it was. I found it in tropical fish shops only a ride away on Glasgow's underground across the Clyde to Cessnock – neon tetras, Siamese fighting fish, red-tailed black sharks, fan-tailed guppies, and the subtle oyster-greys of the kissing gouramis. I found it at the Odeon Cinema at Anniesland in *Mr Magoo* and *Roadrunner* cartoons. And I found it at the University baths, I found it especially and gloriously at the university baths, the blue expanse of the swimming pool against the clean, cream tiles – broader than any colour field painting, a bigger splash than Hockney would ever paint. At art school I revelled in colour but hated the drawing classes. Later I would come to love drawing for its rigour, structure and sheer difficulty. But as a teenager with a mind full of social issues – Vietnam, Biafra, Vietnam, apartheid, ecology, Vietnam – drawing, for a while, was the domain of the enemy: tonal values, sticks of charcoal and conte; cross hatching with HB pencils; aerial passages; the bone beneath the skin. No colour allowed. My attendance at drawing class, I honestly regret to say, was so bad as to be almost invisible. I would stay in my bed-sit and paint. Come the end of the year I passed sculpture, and textiles, and painting, and graphics, and photography, and three-dimensional design, and about six other subjects. But I failed my drawing – not surprisingly – and had to repeat the whole year. My attendance got worse, as did the wars in Vietnam and Biafra, which probably occupied more of my waking thoughts than did copying fake Renaissance statues.

Towards the end of my second year, as spring turned to summer, my life took a significant change in direction. And it happened through a chance meeting at the Tavern Bar.

It was that time of a Friday night when the merriment was really just beginning and the hour hand of the clock was approaching ten, which meant closing time and last orders. Everyone was trying to buy carry-outs to take on to parties, dances, or just back to bed-sits in small groups. 'Eight cans of McEwans Export,' I shouted for the umpteenth time at a passing barman, but it was lost amidst the din. 'Eight cans of . . .' I tried again, standing on tip-toe to bring me up to shoulder height with the competition, but it was like being in a crush at a football match and trying to get the time off the referee. It was hopeless, and I could see my friends Lincoln, Albi, and Jogg weren't having any more success than me. I decided to duck up the street to Frew's Bar on the corner, gloriously free of art students, and buy my provisions there.

Once purchased, I couldn't get back into the Tav and waited around amongst clusters of others for my pals to emerge. With my armful of cans I joined May, Chris and Kath, three of the most alluring pre-Raphaelite beauties, who watched over my antics like concerned big sisters – usually rightly concerned. They were chatting with a few others on the subject of 'the ideal job'.

'What would you most like to do Peter?' May asked me.

'What d'you mean?'

'If you could choose any job at all, anything in the whole wide world.'

'I'd be a lighthouse keeper,' I replied, quick as a flash. 'I've always wanted to be a lighthouse keeper.' It was true, next best thing to being a spaceman, probably better.

And all of this might have been just another conversation borne on the wind and scattered in the darkness of the Hawkhill Road, if it had not been for May coming into the life-drawing class the following Monday (and me even more surprisingly being there) with an advertisement from Saturday's *Scotsman* newspaper seeking full-time lighthouse keepers.

'Why don't you write to them,' she encouraged, 'and see if they take students on for the summer?'

And so I did.

The Interview

I remember with great clarity the day in late spring when I received the letter summoning me to Edinburgh for the interview for the position of relief lighthouse keeper.

I was living in an old house on Dundee's Perth Road which had been split into bedsitting rooms. It was situated diagonally opposite the art school so what I saved on travel I made up for in extra sleep, often until well past noon. The house was occupied by fifteen different art students, their lovers, pets and occasionally children. The name 'Greenfield House' was inscribed in faded gilt letters on the glass panel above the front door. In some quarters it is still as famous as Picasso's early gaff, the 'Bateau Lavoir'.

The house was constantly full of visitors, coming and going, at all hours of day and night. Lincoln lived in the room above me; Albi Sinclair was directly underneath; and Euan Heng right opposite. During one long summer two elderly house breakers rented Albi's room from our landlady (a rather grand dame who looked like Barbara Cartland and ran a string of antique shops along the Perth Road) while he was away and nicked my Fidelity stereo record player which was my most essential possession. It was eventually returned to me, and they to Perth prison.

There was a strange and regular visitor who had befriended the only non-art student in Greenfield House, a civil engineer at the university. We nicknamed this visitor 'The Harbinger of Doom'. He had a thin, weasel face, an equally thin tie, short hair (unlike the rest of us) and chain smoked Gauloises cigarettes. It was rumoured that he owned a gun and it was known, through a nursing friend of Albi's, that he had worked as a mortuary attendant. Whenever he climbed the stairs he kept very close to the walls and seemed to merge in and out of the shadows. Equally exotic, but far more intellectually stimulating, was a friend from Jogg's school days called Duncan, who later became an investigative journalist. In the early Seventies he was in trouble with the forces of law and order himself for making free phone calls to far flung parts of the globe by using secret British Telecom numbers. I also remember, over large mugs of Nescafé and to the backdrop of George Harrison's *Bangladesh*, Duncan talking at great length about some book called *Beneath the City Streets*. I had met my first conspiracy theorist.

But he was only one of many remarkable characters who entered the hallowed hallway of Greenfield, as the house was generally known.

And in that hallway, sitting on cracked linoleum that in its old age looked more like the mosaic tiling it was originally supposed to imitate, sat a large wooden table on which was dumped all the mail of the day. Fifteen sets of bank statements, grant cheques, letters from home, and postcards from abroad were mixed in with at least as many other names of past residents who had long since left Dundee for Sydney, New York or Ullapool.

I have always enjoyed getting mail and that particular day was a very good mail day for me. Since becoming a student with my own postal address I had taken to ordering sundry items from the weekly magazine *Exchange and Mart*. As a boy I had always longed to be able to send off for the X-Ray specs regularly advertised inside American *Spiderman* and *Green Lantern* comics, and better still to earn the ten cents a copy promised for making home deliveries. By my late teens I had graduated away from the world of X-Ray specs (I remember they were often shown alongside a well-dressed girl whose bikini was magically visible beneath her summer dress) but only as far as knee-length leather motorcycle boots, a precaution against Dundee's roving gangs of skinheads and ideal for the art student with no form of transport other than his feet. Then there were the early design solutions to the flat-pack bookcase, again courtesy of *Exchange and Mart*, which I eagerly assembled and filled with my collection of underground magazines such as the infamous schoolkids' *Oz*, well-thumbed copies of *International Times*, and of course all my poetry books.

Various strange boxes came in the mail that day. It was not until I had covered the floor of my bedsit with torn wrapping paper and brown string that I noticed amongst my newly acquired set of non-stick pans and a Venetian gondolier's shirt, the smallest of envelopes addressed to me in a copper-plate script. I turned it over and was puzzled to see the crest of a lighthouse on the back flap, slightly embossed with thin black lines signifying beams of light.

I tore it open, and there was the reply to my query of several weeks ago in which I had asked whether students were ever employed as lighthouse keepers during the long summer months.

Please come to an interview it said, and I noticed with alarm the suggested date was only three days away. We will pay your return fare to Edinburgh, it coaxed, and sure enough there was a tiny claim form, hand-typed, attached with a small gold paperclip.

I scornfully threw my gondolier's shirt in the bottom of my wardrobe and went out to buy a pipe.

The train journey from Dundee south to Edinburgh is one of the world's great railway adventures. It only takes about an hour, but in that time you journey across two astonishing feats of engineering. First there is the Tay Rail Bridge, darkly curving across the silvery river far below. Then there is the jagged coast-line of The Kingdom of Fife that leads towards the great red-oxide giant of the Forth Rail Bridge. This is more impressive in a laid-back horizontal sort of way than the Eiffel Tower and has the added advantage of being functional, this being Scotland after all. I settled down with anticipation as the train pulled out of Dundee station, past the Queen's Hotel, past the back of Greenfield House with the Duncan of Jordanstone College of Art rising above it. I had with me a Tunnock's Caramel Log, a can of Irn Bru, and a copy of the latest *Mad* magazine. As I peeled back the red and gold foil wrapper from my chocolate bar I wondered to myself – and not for the first time – just who the hell 'Duncan of Jordanstone' had actually been? In my two years at the art school no one had ever been able to tell me.

I knew who William McGonagall was. The stumps of the first rail bridge just in view far below us reminded me of him and the disaster he immortalised a century before. I must have taken the train across the Tay Bridge many hundreds of times in my life and each time the opening lines of McGonagall's *The Tay Bridge Disaster* rise up to haunt me, and probably many of the other passengers:

> Beautiful Railway Bridge of the Silv'ry Tay!
> Alas, I am very sorry to say
> That ninety lives have been taken away

On the last Sabbath day of 1879,
Which will be remember'd for a very long time.

It is often claimed that McGonagall is the world's worst poet – but if that is as bad as it gets we shouldn't complain. Indeed, the good people of Dundee often celebrate their local hero with McGonagall Suppers on the very night the rest of Scotland is tucking into their haggis and neeps at the more conventional Burns Suppers in praise of our other national poet, Rabbie Burns.

As a nineteen-year-old I prepared for job interviews with the same spirited disinterest as I prepared for examinations, and once over the Tay Bridge was soon absorbed in my *Mad* magazine while some of the most stunning scenery in the world rushed by. Never mind, I would catch it on the way back.

Edinburgh is one of Europe's most impressive cities to enter by train. You leave the subterranean darkness of the platform area at Waverley Station and walk up a gently rising ramp into a rectangle of bright daylight which might double as a Richard Turrell light sculpture. Then comes the moment near the top when the sky is squeezed out by the mass of Edinburgh Castle perched many hundreds of feet above Princes Street Gardens. In the foreground, the world's largest monument to a literary figure, the Scott Monument, pierces the clouds like a Gothic rocket. Magic, I thought to myself as I dodged the traffic and skirted round the perimeter of Jenners department store, Edinburgh's answer to New York's Bloomingdales, London's Harrods, or Sydney's Grace Brothers.

It was not until I was strolling along George Street in the warm sunshine looking for the home of The Commissioners of the Northern Lights that my thoughts finally turned to lighthouses and the men who run them.

If truth be known, I'd never really *thought through* what a lighthouse keeper actually did.

But I did know it was something I had always wanted to do, whatever it was. Even as a very young child when I turned over various occupations in my mind, as I think everyone does – detective, doctor, trapeze artist, chemist, painter, captain of industry, soldier, tramp, second-hand-bookshop-owner, whisky priest, politician, teacher, spy . . . even then, at the age of four or five, being a lighthouse keeper or being an astronaut were the two professions which really stood out as being a bit special.

In the middle of George Street I found what I was looking for. High above me on the lintel of a building still dressed in the soot of the industrial revolution, I saw a virgin white statue of a lighthouse. I climbed the well-worn stone steps and pushed open the heavy black door. If ever there was a rite of passage, this was it.

'Ello luv, come in,' said a friendly woman with a Liverpool accent who sat behind a large reception desk. She looked like Jane Asher and sounded like Cilla Black. Her white PVC raincoat hung from a hook beside an imposing grandfather clock which chimed loudly three times as the door banged behind me. Postcards from all over the world, many featuring lighthouses, covered a green pinboard on the wall behind her. 'Take a seat thur, luv. You'll be Mr Donaldson's three o'clock. Yer here fur an interview, luv?'

'Yes, lighthouse job,' I said, trying to sound confident, man of the world, fingering the pipe in my pocket as if it was some Pacific Island amulet. I really would have to grow a beard, I decided.

'I'm just a temp. I gerr-all-over town so I do,' she continued in a mesmerising sort of way.'Me Mam calls me The Rash because of the way I spread meself about between jobs, but everybody else calls me Rosie. You know I've been here three weeks an' I still haven't met a lighthouse keeper. Always fancied the outdoor type, so I hav.'

I may have opened my mouth to say something but she talked with such speed it would be like trying to throw pebbles through the spokes of a racing bicycle. But I liked her, I liked her a lot. It was still very trendy to have a Liverpool accent in the early Seventies. Liverpool had been my first choice of art school and I even lived there for ten days before getting a 'late acceptance' from Duncan of Jordanstone. On my first night in Liverpool I had seen *The Scaffold* play in a production called *Mr Plod* at the end of which the whole theatre audience was invited up on to the stage to shake hands with the cast and be presented with a PC Plod badge. I found it the other day in an old shoe box with other such memorabilia as a flyer about Allen Ginsberg's visit to Glasgow and the stub of a ticket for a Rolling Stones concert. Rosie's accent brought it all back in even sharper focus.

While she typed and answered occasional phone calls I immersed myself in the pages of the previous Christmas edition of *The Northern Lighthouse Journal* which lay amongst a pile of old copies of *Punch* and *The Readers' Digest*.

I flicked through grainy black and white images of a myriad of lighthouses, each of a type yet each as individual as erect penises in a porn magazine. Some were tall and slender, others had big knobbly heads and prominent rims, while others were short and thick. I eventually started to read the General Manager's forward. It was a jolly piece obviously aimed at boosting morale and began:

'One of the lines of "Que Sera", the pop number which hit the charts quite a few years ago, was "the Future is not ours to see" and who is going to argue with that? Who, for instance, could possibly have foretold this time a year ago, when the PHAROS, POLE STAR, and HESPERUS were busy laying buoys beside oil rigs and wellheads on newly discovered oilfields, that by Christmas we should be drawing coupons for petrol rationing? It just goes to show that like getting 24 points on the Pools, it is the unexpected that turns up, guard against it how we will.'

He sounded a friendly cove and I was just getting into his head when Rosie shouted across at me in her full scouse accent:

'Mr Donaldson won't keep you long, luv. Ever such a nice man is Mr Donaldson. Such a shame his parents gave him Donald as a first name too, I always think.' What was she talking about? Buzzing away like a scouse chainsaw. 'Seemingly it was his mother's father's name and it was a sort of family thing to do to call the first son Donald. But he's ever such a nice man.'

And indeed he was. I dropped *The Northern Lighthouse Journal* onto the side table just as a clean-shaven man in an elegantly striped shirt and dark trousers, who looked a little bit like the youthful Edward de Bono, appeared before me. He shook hands and ushered me upstairs to his office.

'Some tea, Mr Donaldson?'

'Thank you, Rosie,' he called behind him as we climbed the green-carpeted stairs. 'And the usual biscuits, plain and fancy, if you don't mind.'

'You must be Peter,' he said in a friendly middle-class accent, the sort that is inbred within the east coast Scottish legal community. 'Take a seat, take a seat,' ushering me in to a large, Edwardian looking office with views down to the distant Firth of Forth, 'I'm Donald Donaldson, personnel.' And he perched on the edge of his desk. 'Don't get to see many lighthouses myself, unless we take the children to the beach. These are my two little ones,' and he pointed to two young earthlings framed in gilt beside his crimson leather blotter.

Well, it was more like a friendly chat than an interview I thought afterwards, not realising of course that his easy manner was extracting far more personal details from me than would any formal interview with half a dozen anonymous administrators in suits. We talked about art and family, we discovered which television programmes we had in common and which newspapers we read – or in my case used to read – the International Times and the Guardian, he the Sun and the Scotsman. How was I doing in my studies, he wondered? Did I like a drink with the lads? Had I any strong or peculiar religious beliefs? And what about girls? Was I dating anyone at the moment?

I rolled a Golden Virginia cigarette, tamped the end on the heel of my motorcycle boots, and filled him in on everything relating to life, the universe and Peter W. Hill.

The only point at which the proceedings took a more serious turn was when he cupped his hands together, leaned towards me (and I can still remember the whiff of Gillette deodorant as I waited expectantly for what I sensed would be a very important question) and asked, 'Now Peter, what are you like as a cook?'

I don't suppose I lie any more than the average person. Occasional small white ones but on a scale of one to ten, with American Presidents up there in the double figures, I am way down in the foothills of the decimal fractions, occasionally scoring a one or a two. I'm just not very good at it. 'Oh what tangled webs we weave, when first we practice to deceive,' just about sums it up. But this occasion was different.

'I really enjoy cooking,' I replied, without blinking an eye-lid although the palms of my hands turned suddenly moist. I didn't elaborate on the fact that this mostly related to half a dozen different variations on preparing toasted cheese – sometimes with onion and chutney, always with tomato and pepper, occasionally – if it was a main meal – with a slice of gammon and pineapple.

'Good, good,' he replied. 'Food is very important on a lighthouse, as I believe it is in prisons and on submarines. Men living in confinement, away from the nurture of their families. No alcohol of course, but three good meals a day. Very important.' He hopped off the edge of his desk as Rosie appeared at the open door with a tray of afternoon tea and biscuits.

'We get a lot of students as relief keepers these days,' he said, and had the good grace not to add that there probably wasn't much to choose between us. He dipped a digestive biscuit into his large white tea-cup and for a moment pondered my long hair, frayed jeans (I used to sit up for hours with a darning needle fraying the ends of my denims until they resembled ankle-length Elizabethan ruffs), and sleeveless brown cord jacket over navy blue, heavy-knitted polo neck jumper. No doubt he was comparing me with the other students he had interviewed recently – the marine biologists, the archaeologists, the English Lit students off to write their first novel, the engineers, each with their own reasons to spend their summers on a lighthouse, but each probably looking very much like me, youngsters disillusioned by the war that still raged in Vietnam, as it had throughout our adolescence every night on television and every morning in every newspaper around what was starting to be called The Global Village. Yet we youngsters of nineteen and twenty were still older than some of the boys and girls sent from America, Australia, and New Zealand to fight in Vietnam and to bomb Cambodia. For what?

There is a reason for everything in this world, I reflected as I left the interview, and in the early Seventies most of the answers were to be found somewhere between Richard Milhaus Nixon and the Grateful Dead.

Aberdeen, sixty miles north of Dundee, was about to become the oil capital of Europe. A little bit of Scotland that would be forever Texas, at least until the black gold ran out. Many people were provided with high-paid work, and many of the young, and not so young, lads who would traditionally have gone into the lighthouse service took to the rigs. Perhaps I owed my success to this dearth of young recruits, but come early June I received another envelope bearing the lighthouse coat of arms, along with assorted packages from trading companies and summer holiday catalogues from *P & O Cruises*. I was faced with a dilemma. The letter was offering me employment as a student relief keeper but they wanted me to start almost immediately.

The problem was that to accept the job would mean missing the end of year examinations – setting up the work, taking it down, facing the music of failure once again. I spoke to the most senior drawing lecturer about this, an elderly and craggy-faced man called James Morrison who was probably all of about thirty-eight. He told me I'd have to choose between a life at art school and a life on the lighthouses. Perplexed, I made an appointment to see Ian Fearn, my other drawing lecturer. He was a gentle and good-humoured man, who looked through my thin but honest attempts at capturing old Kate on the life class podium in 3H pencil, and then looked across at me with my waist-length hair and anti-apartheid T-shirt and wisely advised, 'You'll probably get a second chance at art school, but this will be your only chance of being a lighthouse keeper. I'd go for the lights if that's what you really want to do.'

And so I did.

Getting There: By Train, Boat and Tractor

There he goes again, I could almost hear my mother thinking as she waved me off on yet another adventure from the front door of our terraced house in Glasgow, while my father looked on knowingly. Two years earlier they had farewelled me as I left for a summer job at Butlins Holiday Camp in Ayr. The next year I was off to Amsterdam, hippy capital of the world, with a large African drum attached to my rucksack. Couldn't play it, but it looked good. So far, I had always returned safely. Often broke and exhausted, but to the relief of my family always in one piece – or perhaps they were really thinking, my God, he's come back *again*.

The island of Arran was the stepping-stone to my ultimate destination, Pladda. Arran is close enough to Glasgow for its high mountains of Beinn Bhreac and Goat Fell to be visible from the top floor of city tenements, and close enough too for day trippers to get there and back and still have time to enjoy its sixty mile coastline. It's a fair size. Yet it is far enough away to feel you are going on a journey, and the sea crossing adds to the sense of adventure. Arran's population more than trebles in the summer months but beneath the day-tripping veneer is a long and bloody history marked by Viking invasions in the eighth century and eventual union with the Scottish nation in 1266.

The most war-like presence you will find there today is the occasional cloud of midges, gram for gram the most savage creature on the planet. If you are unlucky enough to encounter these fierce-biting insects you would probably gladly swap them for a boat-load of Scandinavian bandits.

I took the train to the mainland point of departure, Ardrossan, with a rucksack full of clothes, books, cassette player and tapes. My selection of sounds included a recently released work called *Tubular Bells*. This strange album seemed to appear from nowhere and to have been overlaid, rather than recorded, by an electronic Mozart called Mike Oldfield. Everyone was buying it, which was not normally how I judged the success of a new album. I tended to be drawn to 'the unusual', as a London madam might describe her kinkier offerings, and liked to think I shared my tastes with about ten other people on the planet. But *Tubular Bells* was different, and doubly attractive for having Viv Stanshall of The Bonzo Dog Band doing the climactic voice-overs at the end. I reminded myself to stock up on more batteries when I reached Ardrossan. Lots more batteries.

There was once a plan to build a canal from Ardrossan to Glasgow, some time round the start of the nineteenth century. It never happened and so Ardrossan never took on the mantle of the 'Venice of the West'. Instead it was gradually globalised out of herring fishing, shipbuilding, coal mining and steel production until its main claim to fame is some of the worst substandard housing in Europe.

I had thirty minutes before the ferry left and bought my batteries in the newsagent on the High Street. Then I purchased a Forfar bridie in the baker's next door. It was time to take to the seas.

As you approach Arran you can see from its profile why it got nick-named 'The Sleeping Warrior'. It lies only fifteen miles from the mainland but sometimes it can be fifteen miles of very rough seas. But the day I caught the ferry it was hot and sunny and the sea was as flat as the sky was blue. Now, it's possible to draw the short straw with the west coast of Scotland and drive there from Croydon or Bath with your buckets and spades and experience nothing but rain for weeks on end. It is also possible that you will get weeks of uninterrupted sunshine and wonder why anyone would bother holidaying in the Mediterranean when all this is on your doorstep . That's the risk you take. If you come to Scotland enough you will experience both extremes. I recommend visiting often and staying long. The summer of 1973 was one of the great ones – hot days and warm summer nights – the sort of climate that got the Bee Gees reaching for their guitars and surfboards and pining for Far North Queensland.

Like every Glasgow school child I was repeatedly told from an early age about the Gulf Stream from Mexico which warms our western coastal waters – unlike the cold east coast cities of Edinburgh, Dundee and Aberdeen. The result was that any time I went near the Clyde as a kid I used to keep my eyes peeled for Mexicans, and once thought I spotted a figure in a sombrero in a distant rowing boat, on a day trip to Helensburgh with my mother and sister. They were not convinced.

Once in Brodick my instructions became increasingly vague. I toyed with the idea of visiting the castle, home of the Dukes of Hamilton. Brodick Castle was once occupied by Oliver Cromwell who added a couple of very plain towers. Later it was given both Gothic and Scottish-Baronial makeovers. But I didn't have time for all that. My now crumpled missive from the Commissioners instructed me to catch a southward bound bus to Lamlash. The night before I had located it on my father's *The Times Map of the British Isles*. Across from it I noticed the tiny Holy Island and a little further down the name Pladda marked by a dot the size of a biscuit crumb. Closer inspection showed it was in fact a biscuit crumb. I scratched it off and found an even smaller dot underneath. *This* was Pladda. It was so small, this dot marking my home for the next two weeks, it could easily have fitted inside the 'P' of the word Pladda, printed in what looked like a six-point font.

In Brodick I lingered over a pint of Export in a harbour-side pub, feeling very much at peace with the world and with myself. With my usual impeccable timing I caught the bus with two minutes to spare and reached Lamlash without a hitch.

Once there I had to catch a taxi from a certain local driver who would know, they promised, the exact spot on the road I was to be picked up by my next connection, a farmer named Harris. I now felt less like a tourist and more like a traveller or itinerant worker. I wandered the streets with my backpack, I asked directions, got lost, found myself again, and some twenty minutes later, having explored various highways and byways, found myself sitting on a white-painted boulder while the taxi driver's wife separated her husband from his vegetable patch. She was a raving beauty. He looked like a butler rejected by central casting for a Hammer horror movie – unbelievably dishevelled in a torn cardigan and with what looked like a sliver of bacon fat hanging from a boil on his lower lip.

'You'll be the student lighthouse keeper,' he said, picking up my rucksack and throwing it in the back of a very old Sunbeam

Talbot. Even by 1970s standards it looked very old, like a black bug made out of very heavy metals. It even had orange indicators that flicked sideways out of the side of the chassis.

'Come on then, son, let's get you to the lighthouse. You're the fifth student keeper I've taken there this year,' he said with a mysterious glint in his eye, and I noticed he was about to drive in his worn carpet slippers. 'And you know, I've never brought a single one back. They do say that the keepers on Pladda are cannibals and on a quiet night you can hear the tortured screams of the young relief keepers just before their throats are cut.'

I must have looked a bit pale, for he punched me on the shoulder and laughed long and hard. 'Dinnae mind me,' he went on. 'They're a fine lot on Pladda. I know them all. You won't want to leave you'll be having such fun. They're real jokers so they are. Finlay Watchorn's on there at the moment. He's mad as a meat-axe. Funnier than Eric Sykes is Finlay. Then there's Ronnie, he's got another week to do. No' got himsel' a wife yet has Ronnie, but he's got a fine wee spaniel for company. An' when I bring Ronnie ashore next week for his holidays you'll maybe get to meet the Professor. He's a local gentleman, a retired school keeper. He's English, but we'll no' hold that against him for he has a very fine manner. Mind you, Duncan the PLK has his religion. He's a Wee Free and Sundays are pretty dull when Duncan's around.'

'What's a PLK?' I asked

'Aye, I can see you've got a lot to learn. A PLK is a Principal Lighthouse Keeper. I've had at least a dozen PLKs in this cab in the past thirty years. If it wasn't for the Northern Lighthouse Board I'd have gone bust years ago.' And he blew his nose hard on a snotty rag.

'That seems like a lot to me,' I replied. 'Why don't they stay longer?'

'Did they not tell you anything at George Street? I presume

they gave you an interview, an' a wee plate of biscuits and some tea? Bet you chatted about everything except how a lighthouse actually works. I know more aboot it than them, an' I just drive a taxi,' he said with a mixture of pride and frustration. 'Civil bloody servants, I ask you. Scunners.' I waited for more enlightenment and he soon continued.

'Look laddie, if you were becoming a full-time keeper instead of being trained up as a student, they would send you to different lights all over Scotland for your first two years. You mightnae visit every light but you'd certainly spend a few weeks on a great many. You'd get to know the service and they'd get to know you.'

I appreciated what he was telling me and kept quiet. I was also trying to hold my breath as the cab smelled like a hamster cage.

'Then you'd get your first real posting,' and his hand swept low towards the horizon to add dramatic effect. 'It might be to a rock, or an island or to a mainland coastal station. Aye, and you'd get a free house for your wife and family on the mainland and all your neighbours would be lighthouse families too.'

I tried to picture it. It seemed bizarre. At that point we were stuck behind a dozen large cows who were slowly being herded across the narrow country road from one field to another.

'But the thing is,' my wise informant told me, 'you only ever spend about three years on the one light and then you are posted to another. Would you like an apple? There's one in the glove box. They did tell you I hope that there is always three keepers on every light? I mean you willnae be there on your tod. In fact, I take it you are here for training since you seem to know sod all about the job?'

'Aye, that's right,' I said, feeling like a real idiot. I dipped into my recent past and offered him a late teenage scowl.

'Well then, there will be four of you, includin' yoursel. The other three will work their normal watches through the night and you just have to watch what they do, learn how tae do it yoursel' . . . Aye Archie, see you in the pub tonight. Set them up for me,' he shouted after the farmer as the last cow disappeared into the field.

'It keeps everybody sane. Three years on a rock off the East Coast, three years up in Shetland, then three on an island in the Hebrides, then doon the west coast. That's the way it goes, something like that. Fine and dandy. And everyone else is changing at different times too. In some ways its toughest for the wives and kiddies. Different homes, new schools, father and husband gone half the year.'

'Why have we stopped?' I asked. We seemed to be in the middle of nowhere.

'This is where you get out, son. There will be a tractor along to pick you up in a minute, or maybe in an hour or two. Hopefully before it gets dark. And watch out for the wolves. There's a lot of sheep gone missing recently, and no one's seen the minister's boy since he went out collecting butterflies.'

He winked at me, and before he could drive off I asked, 'What do you mean a tractor will be along?'

'Tam Harris is your man. He owns all these sheep that ye see, and keeps a few more on Pladda itsel'. He's done a deal with George Street. He's your ferryman farmer and in return he gets the grazing rights to Pladda. Not that there's much there, but enough to feed a few hungry sheep.' And with that he was gone.

Suddenly there was a great silence around me, then gradually I heard the country sounds, the whirring of dragonflies, the cry of a lamb, and the distant sounds of the sea as an oyster catcher screamed.

I settled down for what might be a long wait, watching the tarmacadam road slowly blister in the heat. I was wearing jeans and a T-shirt and everything else was in my rucksack. The air smelled of summer. I leaned against the dry stone dyke and saw that a small burn was running through the field to the distant sea. It reminded me of a poem I knew I had with me in an anthology of American poetry. I'd brought a few poetry books with me, my current favourite being *Poems from Poetry and Jazz in Concert* which I had read at least a dozen times.

I rolled a cigarette and rummaged around for a Mars bar which I thought I'd better eat as it was beginning to liquefy in its wrapper. Still, it hadn't leaked on to my poetry books. I pulled out the American anthology and found the poem I wanted. I had been planning this moment. It is something that artists seem to do. I remember a documentary about the painter David Hockney and his life in California. He talked about how when he drives from coast to desert he always plays a certain operatic tape in his car and times it so that the musical climax happens just as he is cresting the top of a hill and the desert landscape with setting sun is revealed below. In a similar vein I had been keeping my eyes peeled for anything that resembled a river. I hopped on to the wall and sitting above what was admittedly just a narrow stream, I began to read a poem by Langston Hughes called 'The Negro Speaks of Rivers'.

I read it two or three times, pausing between each reading and surveying the land and the sea before me. At that age I didn't know such moments were called sublime, but the experience was no less sublime for my ignorance. On my third reading I sounded the words out loud – 'I bathed in the Euphrates when dawns were young. I built my hut near the Congo and it lulled me to sleep . . . My soul has grown deep like the rivers' – and was only dimly aware of the puttering of a tractor close by. This would be the terror element of the sublime just arriving. When the engine switched off I looked up. I saw before me a very big man, probably in his fifties, standing astride a Massey Ferguson tractor.

'Don't tell me they've sent another fucking hippy!' were his first words to me. 'Hop on then, John Lennon. We'll make a man o' you yet. But it'll be a challenge, I can see that. They call me Big Tam, by the way – Tam Harris' and he crushed so hard my hand within his own that I thought blood would shoot from the fingertips. He continued shaking it for about twenty seconds. Under the pretence of returning my book to the rucksack I felt for fractures but was confident there were only bruises.

'Once you've throttled a few geese you'll be able to shake hands like a man. Now, throw your gear in the trailer and jump in after it,' he ordered, starting up the engine again. He was a dead ringer for one of the characters illustrated in Spike Milligan's classic book *Puckoon*.

For the next five minutes I was thrown about amidst a soup of farmyard detritus – loose straw, several potatoes, earth and sand. I didn't see us cresting the far edge of the field and beginning our rough descent to the little jetty. I was clinging on to the sides of the trailer and trying not to breathe in too much of the dust cloud that covered me while my bones bounced about randomly.

'Out you get,' he ordered again. And when I did it was like arriving in Paradise. Blue waters stretched from a sandy beach out to a little island that seemed so close you could reach out and touch it. At one end was a lighthouse, sitting on the highest point. It looked magic.

'That's your home for the next few weeks,' he said, untying a small rowing boat and throwing a bundle of newspapers into it.

He ordered me to hop in.

And so I did, but it was more of a stumble. Like being drunk without alcohol. Euphoric, that's the word. Harris landed opposite me with a thump and a roll and we pulled out to sea.

And so it was that the farmer-ferryman rowed me across the bay in silence. There wasn't a ripple on the water except for those made by his slowly sweeping oars. I sat transfixed. A seal broke the surface beside us and barked loudly. I swear it guided us in to the island, looking round occasionally to check we were following. I felt like a character in a Rupert Bear book and would not have been surprised if a whistling flying fish had cartwheeled past.

And as we approached the island, in the midday sun, I could see the silhouette of three keepers and a dog. This, I thought with a mixture of excitement and trepidation, was it. There's no going back now.

PLADDA:
LEARNING THE
ROPES

The Mysteries of the Light Chamber

In 1973 there was a shortage of lighthouse keepers. This was not because the lights were being automated – that would come later – but because most of the young men who would traditionally have entered the service were finding better wages building and manning oil-rigs in the North Sea.

The three new colleagues who greeted me on the jetty were from a different generation, in fact several different generations. One was in his sixties and clutched a black bible in his potato-like fist. Another was middle-aged and wiry. The third, Ronnie, in his thirties, had a little cocker spaniel by his side, and was one of the few bachelors I met during my time on the lights. He often blamed the dog for making it difficult to form a lasting relationship with a woman, but I never could see the connection. Nearly thirty years later, in a bar in the magical Orkney Islands, I would meet an ex-keeper who told me Ronnie had eventually married the switchboard operator from lighthouse headquarters in Edinburgh and was, to boot, supremely happy.

How I appeared to them, at first glance on that summer's day in 1973, I can only speculate. I put the groaning sound I heard on arriving down to the old wooden jetty and the swelling sea, but on reflection it probably came from my fellow keepers who saw before them a miniature version of Neil Young from his Crazy Horse period. They probably shared a vision of the light first ceasing to turn then gradually fading to darkness as I lay stoned on the upper rim of the light listening to Van Morrison on my battery-powered cassette recorder while the Oban fishing fleet crashed into the rocks below.

Three of us and the dog hopped on to an old trailer while the Principal Keeper started up the brand new Massey Ferguson tractor, my second in less than an hour, and pulled us up a steep hill to the lighthouse. To my relief I found that the tower of the light was surrounded by numerous out-houses in which I would live, eat, and sleep for the foreseeable future. Later, I would hear tales of other lights, such as the legendary Skerryvore where the keepers lived in the tower itself. In these, the bedroom walls were cylindrical, and there was a circular hole in all the floors and ceilings to allow the enormous metal weight which turned the giant reflectors to be winched up and down at thirty minute intervals throughout the night.

But these and many other stories were all up ahead. Stories told at two in the morning as one watch *sashayed* in to another while deep sleep struggled with reluctant consciousness. Stories told by my elders which served the dual purpose of keeping me awake and teaching me the workings of the light. Stories accompanied by endless pots of tea and sweet digestive biscuits topped with orange Cheddar cheese.

In a strange, slow-motion blur I remember, on my arrival at Pladda, first being shown a tiny bedroom by one of the keepers. I left my worldly possessions on the narrow single bed. The bathroom and toilet, three times the size of my room, lay off a short corridor. Then it was in to the living room for proper introductions, starting with Comet the Spaniel. His master, Ronnie, was an Assistant Lighthouse Keeper (ALK). He had a jolly, pink scrubbed face and a friendly manner. He in turn introduced me to Principal Lighthouse Keeper Duncan McLeish, and Assistant Lighthouse Keeper (ALK) Finlay Watchorn. Hands were firmly shaken across the confined space of the living room with a clashing of pullover sleeves and bulbous knuckles like some weird move in a Morris dance. 'Fit-like, grand ey?' someone enquired incomprehensibly, while someone else squeezed my hand like a lemon and my lungs filled with a mixture of twenty different blends of pipe tobacco that hung like a Los Angeles smog a little above the chair backs.

My first impression of the room was of a lounge and kitchen combined. A table with four places was already set for a meal. A grandfather clock stood guard at the point where the living area with its upholstered armchairs met the little kitchen with sink and stove. I remember a kettle was bubbling quietly on the gas rings. Finlay Watchorn went across to it, lifted its round hooked handle with a white dishcloth and added more water to it. He didn't prepare a teapot, as I expected, but merely returned the kettle to the stove.

During my two weeks of training the beacon above us would be switched on and off fourteen times, but the gas below the kettle, I soon learned, was never dimmed. Like the flame of the unknown soldier it burned, and the kettle simmered, twenty-four hours a day, three hundred and sixty-five days a year. Everyone on Pladda was addicted to tea.

'I'm chust going to do the weather,' Duncan said to the others in his slow Hebridean lilt. 'Tell the laddie about the routines.'

'He's just gone to make a weather report and call up Corsewall,' Ronnie explained mysteriously. 'You'll soon pick up the routines,' he said. 'Piece of cake.'

'Thank you,' I replied.

'Nah, nah, I'm no offering you cake, eedjit, I mean the routines are complicated but soon learned. Now, while Duncan's away we should tell you that he is a very religious man and we all respect that. He'll want to say grace at every meal except breakfast, and he disappears to his room all day Sunday, except when he's on duty.'

'We never make fun of a man's religion on the lighthouses,' Finlay Watchorn continued Ronnie's remarks, scratching his bearded chin with the stem of his pipe. I remember the taxi driver who took me across Arran had compared him to Eric Sykes, but to me he looked more like Captain Haddock from the Tin Tin books. 'You'll soon discover that we make fun of just about everything else, but no' a man's religion. Now let's think about some lunch,' and he rubbed his hands together. 'I'm on lunches this week.'

Ronnie was bouncing a red ball for Comet, and as I turned round to see the dog jump and catch it between his teeth Finlay turned on the television set.

'Let's see what's happening in the great outdoors. We aye watch the one o' clock news before we settle down for lunch,' he explained.

This was a novelty for me. During my two years as an art student I don't think I'd bought a single newspaper and never possessed a television set. My recent television diet had been my weekly trip with my mates Lincoln, Albi, and Jogg to watch *Colditz* in the flat of Marion and Fionna, two good friends in third year who lived above a fish-and-chip shop on Dundee's Peddie Street. Like many of my generation the war in Vietnam had weighed so heavily on my mind and disillusioned us about the 'straight' world that we'd sought to form an alternative world of our own. During my months on the lighthouses I found I was rejoining a shared reality, filling in the many gaps in recent history and what was soon to be called 'popular culture', an overly-academic term for entertainment, I've always thought.

The set took a few minutes to warm up, as they did in those days. Then immediately we were beamed live by satellite to the Watergate hearings in Washington.

'Och, it's no John Dean again?' Finlay feigned dismay. 'Bring on Tricky Dicky and yon Kissinger. Let's hear what they have to say. Nail the bastards.'

I suddenly experienced the bizarre image of lighthouse keepers all around the globe, thanks to recent satellite technology, from Tierro del Feugo to Nova Scotia, being able to tune in on a daily basis to the world's biggest political circus. It was rather cumbersomely known as The Senate Select Committee on Presidential Practices, but school kids and their grandparents from Paris to Peru knew it simply by its rather poetic tag of 'Watergate'.

And as we tuned in Ronnie shouted advice, admonition and encouragement back at the main players on the black-and-white television set. Over the next few days I witnessed how Ronnie interacted with the television in this way no matter what was on. It didn't matter if it was *Emmerdale Farm*, *The Generation Game*, *Star Trek*, or his favourite *Skippy the Bush Kangaroo* – they all got Ronnie's wisdom or rebuke.

As we joined them from Pladda, John Wesley Dean III was getting the third degree from Sam Ervin Jr, chair of the committee. The camera closed in on Dean who was saying, 'I do not know whether Attorney General John Mitchell approved the Watergate wiretapping operation.'

'Pull the other one,' Ronnie told him, wagging his finger at the screen. 'Of course ye knew about it. You all did. You were up to your armpits in it.'

'Now, now,' Finlay admonished, 'What about the presumption of innocence?'

I listened agog as Dean continued dropping metaphorical bombshells from another time zone with the same easy manner that Kissinger dropped real ones on the peasants of Cambodia. 'It was the President who ordered the 1971 burglary of the psychiatrist's office in Los Angeles,' Dean protested. 'They were looking for information about Daniel Ellsberg in relation to the Pentagon papers.'

At this point Duncan rejoined us from 'doing the weather', whatever that meant. John Dean was babbling on about Egil Krogh and the Plumbers, which I thought sounded like an ace name for a rock band or a James Bond villain. 'Switch that rubbish off,' Duncan commanded like an old testament prophet. 'It is time to eat the food that the Good Lord has provided for us, courtesy of 84 George Street.'

'Purvey time,' Finlay Watchorn winked at me. 'You sit yourself there, Peter. Our first course today is vegetable soup.'

Half a gallon of soup divided between four people is still about a pint each, and that is what we consumed along with a whole loaf of sliced white bread.

Mind you, the sea air had given me an appetite, and although I finished last, I did finish.

As I was licking my soup spoon clean and thinking to myself that that would keep me going nicely until tea time, Finlay was lifting what turned out to be a huge lamb casserole from the oven.

'I'll give you a hand with the rice,' Ronnie offered, and before I knew it I was tucking into a meal that would have easily fed me for a week back in my student bedsit in Greenfield House.

As we ate, the wit and wisdom of my three new friends increasingly reduced me to tears of laughter as they ribbed each other on every aspect of their lives and coaxed me to join in.

'Ronnie comes from just outside Perth, Peter,' Finlay Watchorn told me. 'But we dinnae hold that against him. What do they call it Ronnie, the Carse o' Gowrie? They tell me Perthshire is a great place for growing mushrooms. They seem to respond well to the dampness and the lack of sunlight. I've never been there myself, thank God.'

'Don't you listen to him, Peter,' Ronnie replied. 'It's a wonderful place, and not a lighthouse for miles. But of course you're from the big city of Dundee, you must know Perth well.'

Finlay excused himself to check on the apple crumble as I squeezed in another mouthful of the most exquisite braised lamb.

'Some more bread, laddie?' Duncan inquired, opening another loaf while Ronnie gave us a run-down on yesterday's edition of *Skippy* and his mates in the bush.

'If you stay in the service long enough,' Ronnie continued the Australian theme, 'you'll meet Ozzie MacGregor. He's on Corsewall just now. Amazing set of boomerangs he's carved from driftwood. Chucks them at the gannets and lets them float back to the beach.'

Over the coming days I witnessed how these three wonderful men could simultaneously carry out three separate conversations for sustained periods of time. Occasionally their quite discreet stories would converge and embrace before going their different ways, only to meet again half an hour down the track.

'Time to do the dishes,' Duncan eventually announced. 'Then we'll have our tea and biscuits.'

I was bloated, the only word for it. I'd managed a small serve of apple crumble and custard, but it seemed a reckless act.

Washing dishes immediately after eating a meal was another

novelty to me. Normally I could go days without washing up, occasionally doing the whole lot in the bath in Greenfield House, one of many tricks I'd learned from Lincoln, my closest art school friend.

We moved to the sink where Finlay washed in what must have been near boiling water while Duncan and I dried. Ronnie put away.

'Watch where he puts them,' Duncan advised. 'We all take turns at doing everything here.'

As we washed and dried they taught me about 'the routine'.

'Normally there's only three of us on a lighthouse,' Duncan spoke slowly and clearly. 'So all lighthouse routines are built around the work being shared between three people. It's very democratic.'

'Except he gets paid more than us,' Finlay joked. 'For doing the same work, like.'

Duncan flicked his dish towel to the side of Finlay's ear and continued.

'If your watch happens just before breakfast, let us say, then you're the man who cooks breakfast that day. But you won't cook it the next day as you will be on a different watch then.' It all sounded very complicated. I usually just grabbed a couple of Weetabix and smoked a Golden Virginia, if I bothered at all.

'If you are on the afternoon watch,' Duncan broke into my thoughts, 'you cook the evening meal that day, but you won't cook it again for another three days.'

'However,' Finlay Watchorn chimed in, swivelling round from the sink, pink rubber gloves up to his elbows. 'The same person cooks lunch all week. Like muggins here this week.'

'So do the other two have the mornings off?' I asked innocently.

'The mornings off?!!' Finlay exclaimed like the Red Queen in

Alice in Wonderland. 'There's no such thing as "the mornings off" on a lighthouse. Och no! Monday to Friday the two other keepers work from nine till one while the third prepares our luncheon banquet. On Saturdays we clean the lighthouse from top to toe.'

'What sort of work?' I wondered aloud.

'Whatever 84 George Street, in their wisdom, tells us to do,' Ronnie said, taking four dinner plates from Duncan and placing them in the old oak sideboard. 'Build a jetty, expand the vegetable patch, re-paint the tower white, put in more vegetables, repair the boat, pull out more vegetables, mend the nets, clean the fog horn, degrease the generator, perhaps a bit of dry stane dyking if it's tae yer liking. I think they have wee competitions at 84 over their tea and biscuits just to see what they can dream up for us to do next.'

'Jacks of all trades we are,' Finlay continued. 'Have you ever sheared a sheep, Peter?'

I scarcely liked to ask what happened on a lighthouse in the afternoons, having so shocked my fellow keepers by suggesting that the mornings might consist of free time. Nobody seemed to be about to do anything other than make a large pot of tea and produce a roll of digestive biscuits and some Cheddar cheese. However, curiosity got the better of me and I asked, 'What are we up to this afternoon?'

'Och, whatever you like, laddie,' Duncan told me. 'You always get the afternoon off on a lighthouse.' And suddenly the idea of writing haikus and painting seascapes rushed back to join me.

'I'm goin' tae ma pit for a sleep,' Ronnie said. 'I was on watch from two till six this morning so I've had less than two hours kip. Time to shoot the crow. I'll be up for *Crossroads*.'

'You'll find that happens every three days,' Duncan added. 'But we've hardly even begun to teach you the routine. I'm on watch from six till ten this evening. You'll join me for that Peter and I'll show you how to light the light and in between times I'll take you through the whole routine' – spoken slowly, liltingly *rooo*-teen – 'If you've finished your tea you should go for a wee walk around our island. That's what I'm going to do. We usually walk on our own. It is a time for our own thoughts and innermost reflections.' I could do wi' some of that, I decided.

I gave Duncan a ten minute head start on his constitutional before going out myself to explore my new home.

All lighthouse keepers have their hobbies. Some build miniature five-masted schooners in bottles. One I knew spent three years building a real motor boat in the vegetable shed behind the fog signal, while others carved mermaids from bits of driftwood, played hymns on the one-stringed fiddle, became experts on the subject of the *Dr Who* television series, or (God bless him) cooked gourmet meals with the lobsters that we caught and the spices that we had flown in by helicopter or delivered by the supply vessel, *The Pole Star*. Others prayed. One frequently gave spirited renditions of the delta blues on the 'moothie'. I never could get mouth-organs to work beyond producing a sequence of random notes that lacked melody, tone, and even discernible rhythm. My efforts sounded like a couple of possums hard at it in a loft, or the orgasmic cries of an asthmatic bull-seal midway between sexual climax and cardiac arrest. So on the lighthouses I read poetry instead, and occasionally tried to write it. That was my hobby. Poetry has always been important to me. There is a poem for every phase of life and at least two for every situation: Dr Seuss, Sylvia Plath, Lewis Carroll, Allen Ginsberg, Les Murray, John Keats, Leonard Cohen, George Mackay Brown, Walt Whitman, Liz Lochhead, Paul Celan, Spike Milligan, Robert Crawford, Hugh McDiarmid, Ivor Cutler ... Some of them are referred to in these pages and you may care to seek them out and enjoy them at your leisure. On other occasions you may just want to open a favourite poetry book at random and pretend you are on a lighthouse. Try staying awake until three in the morning and you will soon find you are so tired you can hardly think. Open your curtains over the black starry night sky above Hampstead, or Boston, or Sydney – wherever you live – and read a favourite poem. Then stare at the sky and contemplate the vastness of the universe. Gradually, you will turn into a lighthouse keeper. But take your time, for time is precious. There's no hurry. There never is on a lighthouse, as my first afternoon on one taught me.

I had just set off on my walk. I was burning off the biggest meal I'd eaten in years. It was a beautiful summer afternoon and a family of seals was guarding the rocks around the bay. Duncan McLeish, as reported earlier, had already gone for his constitutional. I strode past him on my way down the little path and gave a cheery wave. The problem was, the island was only about half the length of a football field and five minutes later I found myself back where I started, wondering where to go next. Duncan, meanwhile, hadn't moved – or at least I thought he hadn't. Apparently, the trick was to walk as slowly as possible and take as long as possible to cover a very small distance. So I slowed down. I used my eyes as much as my legs. I picked up pebbles and turned them over in my hand. Like Blake, I saw a universe in a grain of sand, and wondered. I breathed the sea air, deep into my lungs. When was the last time I enjoyed the natural sounds of the daylight hours without traffic noise of some sort in the background? Perhaps never, not even on a mountain top where a Christian Salvesen lorry always appears on the winding road below to break the spell. This was pre-industrial. Damn near medieval . . . except for the technology of the light itself. But there have been beacons of one kind or another for thousands of years, from Alexandria to Arbroath. I watched the oyster catchers dance like mechanical toys.

Replete is the only word for the way the huge lunch had left me feeling. And contented. I liked it here and looked forward to learning more about 'the routine'.

As a hybrid art student-cum-hippy I had long scorned routine: waking when I chose, working till dawn, eating irregularly, making no plans and always acting on the spur of the moment. I was a sucker for the moody, self-obsessed poetry of Hermann Hesse:

'Often I tried the frightening way of "reality,"
Where things that count are profession, law, fashion, finance,
But disillusioned and freed I fled away alone
To the other side, the place of dreams and blessed folly.'

After only a few hours on Pladda I was getting the first inklings that perhaps I could tire of that old way of life. Perhaps there was another – not better, but different – way of living.

Gradually, as days went by, the outer wall of the lighthouse compound would appear a fair distance away from our living quarters and to walk to the far end of the island required considerable planning and possibly sandwiches and a thermos of coffee. I have an artist friend called Douglas Gordon who once slowed down Alfred Hitchcock's *Psycho* until it lasted all of twenty-four hours. To see three lighthouse keepers out for a stroll on Pladda was to see a similar rupturing of the space-time continuum.

'Aye, you'll have to remember you're not in the big city any more,' Duncan advised me that first evening, looking up from a psalm he was reading in the bible that always seemed to accompany him, and adding cryptically, 'Grant that this day we fall into no sin, neither run into any kind of danger.'

I must have looked puzzled, for he added, with a wink, 'You will find that we do no running on this island, and when we walk we do so at a very slow pace.'

'Yes, of course,' I replied.

'And one other thing. No whistling on the Sabbath.'

I strolled off as slowly as I could to inspect the vegetable patch, wondering what Duncan would say when he heard my Jimi Hendrix compilation tape that I had been dying to play all day. I had lugged my portable tape recorder, miniaturised to roughly the size of a big city phone book (that was the state of the art in 1973), all the way from Dundee on the opposite coast of Scotland. I planned to play the maestro's rendition of 'The Star-Spangled Banner' across the still waters of the Firth of Clyde at the earliest opportunity.

How can I describe it? I've often said that being on a lighthouse resembled nothing more than being in a spaceship. Perhaps a spaceship co-designed by NASA and the Goons.

And as if in agreement with this sentiment, while Watergate, Vietnam, and Brezhnev's visit to America clogged the television news during my two weeks on Pladda, high above us three Skylab astronauts struggled with the daily routines that we all took for granted. We watched them trying to complete ordinary tasks in zero gravity as slices of bread and ruptured tomatoes floated around them. Living in confined space and good comradeship was perhaps our greatest commonality. By contrast, we had it easy. We had our comfy armchairs, our Tetley tea bags, our lively repartee, and our coal fires. But we also had the night sky, the *aurora borealis*, and the luxury of leaning on the rail at three in the morning, high above the sea swell, watching satellites track across the Milky Way. And I would smile a secret smile to myself in the absurd knowledge that I was actually being paid to stargaze.

Yet the wild nights, when they happened, weren't so easy when, with gale-force winds and a spume-tanned face, I'd have given anything to be inside a warm, dry spaceship rather than outside on the rim of the light, knuckles white as if the bone beneath were shining through . . . out on the rim, out on the rim, out on the rim . . . I would repeat the words as I pulled myself round, checking on the other lights. It was as if all my senses were being assaulted by the universe – the wind trying to rip off my ears and blow through my ear drums with the savagery of an apple corer; my tongue marinaded in the sharp salt spray; my fingers, keep them moving, lest they froze against the metal rail, and the paraffin vapour rising through my nostrils like a giant wave while all my eyes could see was blackness spangled with a field of expanding stars as if the sky had turned into a huge Ross Bleckner canvas. Cold, and wet, and aching in every muscle, I would pull the heavy door fast behind me and shoot the submarine-like bolt against the bulkhead. And in the warmth of the light chamber the three-in-the-morning tiredness would be released like the most narcotic perfume. The fight from then onwards was to stay awake and retain consciousness for another three hours.

Ronnie used to joke that on Skerryvore, far to our West, where the keepers lived in the tower for most of their term of duty, it was possible to be seated at the dining room table and from there perform most tasks without leaving your seat. You could lean across and pluck the kettle from the stove. You could make a radio broadcast to the mainland. Or take a Yorkshire pudding from the oven. You could turn on the television and watch your favourite soap opera. He even claimed you could wash and dry the dishes without having to rise from your seat.

In the early days of my apprenticeship it was difficult to know when I was getting my leg pulled, precisely because so much of what sounded far-fetched eventually proved to be correct. Stories I heard on one lighthouse would be confirmed months later on a different light with a different crew.

This shared camaraderie contrasted with our internal lives, our solitary thoughts, our three in the morning musings, and especially our readings. Having read and re-read most of J. R. R. Tolkein and Herman Hesse I graduated around this time to Kurt Vonnegut and Carlos Castenada. Vonnegut was a particularly sane companion to have on a lighthouse and a fine contrast to the madness of Vietnam. So at three in the morning I would pick up classics such as *Cat's Cradle* and read sections at random. I particularly enjoyed Bokonon's 'Fifty-third Calypso' and read it many times that summer from the rims of three different light-houses. I felt it captured the beauty and absurdity and complexity of this awesome planet where 'A Chinese dentist and a British Queen' all had to fit together 'in the same machine', a feeling aided by the visual backdrop of the night sky and the knowledge that I was the only sentient being awake for miles around.

It is easy from a distance of over a quarter of a century to forget what happened on which lighthouse, or who told what tale in the depths of the night. Perhaps it was because the keepers on Pladda made such an impression that recollections of the island itself, and of the light, are hazier. The next two islands I was posted to are far clearer, but on them I had less to learn. I seem to recall that there were actually two lighthouses on Pladda, immediately adjacent to each other. I think they belonged to different centuries and that it was the smaller of the two which was currently in use. I feel frustrated that I cannot remember such an obvious thing, while the outpourings of the television come with almost instant recall.

Then there were the fog signals. Again, I cannot remember

which type of signal was on each island. And yet, as I type, gradually it is coming back. Some were massive steam driven things occupying whole sheds. They looked like a cross between a Tibetan horn (if you've read *Tintin in Tibet* you will be able to picture it) and a Tinguley sculpture. The older ones more than nodded in the direction of Heath Robinson's quirky machines. Others were sleek and modern like a bank of fire sirens. Either way, they were hell to live with when in operation.

Memory is strange. Largely, it is my early days on Pladda that remain with me most vividly. Everything was new to me and I had to take copious notes to remind me what had to be switched on or off, when and how. I still have those notes in a kind of on-running diary I had been keeping since I was about sixteen. In those days, Woolworths in Byres Road, the main artery in the West End of Glasgow, sold packs of three spiral-bound yellow notebooks, each pack not much bigger than a packet of cigarettes and thin enough to slip in a shirt pocket. I must have gone through dozens of them, scribbling poetry, making sketches for paintings, jotting down daily events.

One such entry, for example, tells me that not long before leaving for Pladda I went to the art school film club. With all the bluntness of a *Spectator* film critic I wrote, and I can hardly believe it now: 'Went with Lincoln, Albi and Jogg to see an Andy Warhol film called *Chelsea Girls*. It was the biggest load of rubbish I have ever had the misfortune to sit through in my entire nineteen years. Talk about boring!!!!!! We tried to get our money back. We did not succeed but went to the Tav instead. Glad I am a painter.'

When I returned to the living quarters that first afternoon I found Ronnie was already starting to prepare the evening meal. His watch was the otherwise invisible one from two in the afternoon till six in the evening. The only other duty in this period was to make a radio and weather check. I could not face even looking at food, so I disappeared to my room and immediately fell into a deep sleep. In that sleep I had the first of many dreams of being surrounded by a flat sea on a sunny summer's day. The light is diamond hard and sharp as a lemon. Strange islands break the surface tension and occasional rowing boats drift past. I realise that my eyes are the eyes of the sea and I am looking all around me. I have no body. I sink to the ocean floor and linger there until the most godawful ringing noise wakes me up. There is a small bell in my room and its size is nowhere relative to its strength. It is of a similar type to the sort of maid's bell found in Victorian terraced houses across what was once ignominiously called the Empire. I rub my eyes and my mouth has that horrible late after-noon post-sleep taste in it. The bell is still ringing but stops abruptly. I look at my watch. It is precisely five o'clock.

I pull on my trousers and shuffle through to the living area. It seems to be teeming with people and is heavy with pipe tobacco. No, there are only my three companions but they seem to be doing so many different things in such a small space that it appears more crowded than it actually is. Duncan is winding the grandfather clock with a large key. 'Come in laddie, come in. I chust thought I'd let you hear what the bell sounds like that will wake you up when it is time for you to begin your watch. You've got a day's work ahead of you before you go back to dreamland.'

'Have you started dreaming about the sea yet?' Finlay Watchorn asked, and I felt like my brain had been robbed. 'It happens to all of us, some sooner than others,' he continued. He was busy sorting through the newspapers and magazines that Harris the ferryman had brought across. 'We all start to dream of the sea, and our dreams soon become like a second home.'

I noticed one copy of the *Sunday Post*, several of *The Times*, a

People's Friend, a small stack of *The Daily Record* from Glasgow, and a copy of *Time* magazine. 'Harris aye brings across our reading material,' Finlay explained. 'His daughter works at the hotel and aye keeps what's left at the end of the day. Once we've read them we use them to light the fire. Then there's the Professor with his damn crosswords.'

Ronnie had obviously got the evening meal under control from the burbling and clicking sounds coming from the stove where several pots of different sizes simmered like a private percussion group. He was washing up the utensils at the sink and craning his head round in an attempt to watch *Daktari* on the BBC. 'No' the hypodermic!' he shouted at the television vet who was in the process of operating on what looked like a baby giraffe. 'You're 'no going to stick that thing in the wee creature?' and Comet, playing at his feet, barked along in sympathy.

I can't remember the details of my second lighthouse meal with the same clarity as the first. There were three courses, as every meal seemed to have, and the middle one involved a lot of meat while the third was over-heavy on sugar. I do remember the novelty of the first course, though, which was freshly caught crab on Jacob's Cream Crackers. Magic. I was beginning to worry about what I would prepare, or more precisely how I would prepare it, when my turn came around – which it would, with the cold inevitability of a revolving light.

'Ronnie caught six of them in his creel,' Finlay explained. 'We'll be eating crab for a few days yet.' I had no problem with that. They were delicious.

Afterwards, with the dishes washed and the jokes all told, each seemed to go their separate way. Finlay was going to be on the watch which began at two in the morning, so he went to bed to get some sleep. Finlay, Duncan explained, would be woken by Ronnie around 1.45 a.m. Ronnie in turn would previously have got in an hour or two's sleep himself and be woken by Duncan and myself around 9.45 p.m. It appeared that Duncan and I were already 'on watch' and he would devote the next few hours, until it was time to light the light, to going over 'the routine' with me in some detail. I excused myself momentarily and went to get one of my little yellow notebooks. I have it in front of me now. The blue ink has faded slightly. It is a little the worse for wear. But all the instructions are still there, as recorded at Duncan's elbow. It begins:

Light Duties –
1) *Turning on the light:*
a) Go up to lightroom and light bunsens
b) Lift out stops
c) Let them soak
d) Turn round and light
e) Place under light at top between cross-sections (leave for ten minutes)
2) *Raise the blinds*
3) *Go down and switch on pumps (turn on numbers 1 to 3 in any order)*
4) *Lighting the light*
a) Light tapir (scribbled note in margin about South American mammal)
b) Turn dial to <u>20</u>
c) Light fumes when they appear (above the light)
d) Remove pan from underneath and blow out flames
e) Empty pan
f) Go down and start turning
5) *Fill in log books*

6) *Remember: When 'off' gear handle is down*
7) *Oil generators and empty waste*

All of these instructions became much clearer when Duncan eventually took me up the stairs of the lighthouse and turned the theory into practice. For the moment, I was still an armchair lighthouse keeper.

Duncan had begun our session by gently encouraging me, in an avuncular way, to stop referring to the four-hour watches we all undertook twice in every twenty four hours as 'shifts'. This lapse was a hangover from my previous summer job working in the Pig and Whistle bar in Butlin's in Ayr, which by strange coincidence was just across the water from where we now conversed. He then went on to give me a brief overview of lighthouses and their upkeep before progressing to the detailed instructions outlined above.

He told me that there are three types of lighthouse: rock lighthouses come straight out of the sea and as a keeper you spend all of your time living, sleeping, and eating in the tower. Coastal lighthouses skirt the British Isles and are on the mainland, allowing keepers to live with their families. Island lights are situated on uninhabited islands. I would eventually work on three of them. A trainee lighthouse keeper entering the job for life would spend 18 months serving short periods of time on many different lights around Scotland, as my taxi driver had tried to explain to me earlier in the day. They would also undergo strict psychological tests before gaining employment as prior to this there had been a few ugly murders and suicides – but Duncan spoke little of those, although others would later.

Thereafter he (and there were sadly never any shes since the job had ceased being a family one many decades ago, when husband and wife teams kept the lights burning) would be posted to a variety of lights for three years at a time. In the space of less than a decade a keeper might find himself on a rock west of the Hebrides, then on mainland Orkney, and after that in an inner-city harbour station like Footdee in Aberdeen.

Each light had three keepers and each keeper took two four-hour watches in every 24 hours. These watches rotated daily.

Let's say you were on from ten at night until two in the morning. You would then sleep until breakfast at eight (always attended by all three keepers) and then from nine until twelve two keepers would perform any duties that needed doing around the island.

During this period the third keeper would prepare the sort of lavish three-course lunch which I had recently enjoyed. Usually it would be eaten at noon or one o'clock depending on the light and the whim of the different keepers. One keeper would be on lunch duties for a whole week while the other two spent the mornings working on whatever '84' decreed needed doing about the place. Your next watch would then be from two until six in the evening but as a daytime watch it was usually a quiet period with only a few radio tests to make to all the nearby lights and coastguard stations. You would then have a night watch, a 'Rembrandt' as I immediately nicknamed them, from two in the morning until six in the morning, the worst of the three since you would be lucky to get an hour's sleep before you had to be up again for breakfast. The following afternoon you would sleep. And so it would go on, seven days a week. The longest I kept up such a regime was eight weeks without a break and I can tell you I was ready for a pint of export and a 'nippy sweetie' when I eventually hit the high-life in Girvan.

We were kept pretty busy. I never did complete many haikus or watercolours. The light had to be wound up like a giant grandfather clock every thirty minutes. Every twenty minutes we checked the air pressure to the paraffin and if necessary pumped it up. This was a subtle ruse to keep us awake and alert, as was the little hammer that banged away on the brass every second through the night – for a lighthouse is nothing if not the most phallic clock in the world. At the highest level the light itself burned and the giant mirrors, the reflectors, turned like a slow-motion merry-go-round supported on a huge bath of mercury. To light the paraffin one had to cause a mini explosion within the light room, allowing a small cloud of paraffin vapour to form in the air, tucking one's face under ones arm for protection while igniting the gas with a burning taper.

Duncan explained that many lighthouses still used paraffin as their source of illumination because the beam was stronger and travelled a greater distance. Increasingly, new forms of electric light were being introduced into the service.

The most magical moments happened when we changed watches. There was an unwritten rule that the keeper about to head off for bed would stay up for an extra half an hour and engage in conversation with his colleague in order to help him stay awake. A large pot of tea would have already been prepared along with a plate of digestive biscuits and cheddar cheese. It was at these times that I really got to know my fellow keepers. One person would be consumed with tiredness, the other trying desperately to shake off his dreams. Magritte would have loved it. It was at that hour in the morning with the wind whistling like a devil outside that I would hear the tales of lighthouse murders and suicides. After bridges, lighthouses are a favourite spot for those who want to take a header from a great height.

Isolation affects people in different ways, and island life can be utterly surreal.

But I'm getting ahead of myself. At this point all these adventures were up ahead and I had still to work through a complete watch.

'Come on, laddie,' Duncan said, looking up at the grandfather clock. 'It's time to light the light.'

Instructions for a Nuclear War

It was still daylight of a late summer's evening when Duncan and I walked the few paces from our living quarters across to the tower. Our first port of call was not the tower itself but the large outhouse next to it which housed the wild beast which made the fog signal scream in agony. Inside, Duncan picked up a large green metal drum which he explained contained paraffin, and then led me slowly up the stairs to the light chamber.

Everything was spotlessly clean. Brasswork shone like warm butter. Sunlight bounced off chrome. There was a small wooden table and two chairs. I felt like a character from *The Borrowers*, shrunk to the size of a mouse and trapped inside a giant clock. There were dials everywhere, but that was just on the surface. Transparent layers were visible underneath – cogs, ratchets, spindles and gear levers.

And above us was a metal walkway with a solid metal ladder leading up to it. I climbed up behind Duncan and felt like I was stepping on to the top of the world – a secret universe contained within a hemisphere of glass.

'The very first thing we do,' Duncan told me, 'is to lift up the blinds. It is a sacking offence to leave the blinds down, just as it is to let the light stand, or worse to go out.' And he went around the dozen or so Bandaid-coloured blinds that surrounded the light chamber, each longer than a trestle table, and released them gently. As they wound up with clatter and spin, the last of the day's light flooded the room. In the middle of the chamber was the light itself, like the giant eyeball of a one-eyed God. It had mirrors for a pupil and reflectors were its cornea. Circular brass rails framed it like a monocle. I had never seen any object quite so beautiful. I stared at it in wonder. It was like being close to a sleeping wild animal with no bars in-between.

'We aye get the light going half an hour before the sun sets,' Duncan explained, leading the way back down to the lower half of the chamber.

'Now, first thing you do is top up the paraffin in here,' and he pointed to what looked like a giant aqualung. He unscrewed a brass lid on a chain, inserted a funnel and poured in a measured amount from the can we had brought with us from below decks.

'Then you pump up the pressure until the needle is at this mark here, see?' I looked. A wooden pump-handle, like a thin rolling pin, sat at right angles to the canister.

'You have a try,' Duncan suggested, and I took the handle in both hands. I was surprised at how much pressure it took and I needed my full strength to work the handle up and down. 'That'll keep you fit through the night. We usually check the pressure every twenty minutes but you dinnae always have to pump it up. Now let's get this thing lit.'

Each lighthouse has its own quite unique mechanism and overall design. My second light, for example, was so large that you had to climb inside it and were surrounded by giant mirrors and reflectors. On Pladda, you could just lean in and turn the necessary knobs and valves. I watched Duncan do just that with matches and taper in hand, instructing as he did so. 'Now this takes some skill Peter, watch carefully,' and I understood from his tone of voice that this was the crucial bit coming up. 'We have to cause a *small* explosion, not a *big* explosion. You only get it wrong once. Slowly turn this dial here and let the paraffin vapour escape. If you don't let enough out it won't light. Too much and . . . well, you want to keep your eyebrows, I'm sure. Now I'm striking the match and lighting the taper.' This he did well away from the vapour before plunging it towards the light. There was a roar and an intense flash that turned from blue to gold and back to a mellow yellow – all in an instant. He then adjusted the flame to the correct brightness.

'We have our light,' Duncan said with some pride. 'But it's just standing still, sending out a single beam in one direction. We have to get her moving now. It is a bit like starting a round-about at a playground for the bairns. You'll see the mercury I was telling you about earlier. If you stand halfway up the ladder like I'm doing and push very hard it'll get itself going and adjust to its own speed.'

'So how does it keep turning all night? Do we have to keep pushing it?' I asked naively.

'Ah, the weights,' Duncan answered mysteriously. 'The weights . . . That's the secret of a lighthouse, the weights. They are attached to the end of a long chain and slowly drop the length of the tower. They take exactly thirty minutes to reach the bottom of the tower, and as they drop gravity keeps the reflectors turning. It really is just like a giant grandfather clock.'

'So how do we wind them up again?' I wondered.

'You're asking the right questions,' Duncan continued. 'We do it with this handle here. It's a little bit like the crank handle on a car to get it going in frosty weather. You can turn this one with one hand, but on some lights it is a two-handed job and requires a lot of strength. On others it is tiny and can be accomplished with just your fingers.'

One of several novels I had brought with me was *The Third Policeman* by the Irish genius Flann O'Brien. Suddenly Duncan took on the air of PC McCruisken whose obsession with mechanical detail verged on, nay exceeded, the insane.

Where there had been utter quiet a few minutes before, now there was noise. The flame roared around the lamp, the ratchets and cogs clicked and clacked, yet the many tonnes of machinery glided silently on their own private ocean of mercury.

'Now, Peter, take a seat for a minute, I want to explain something important to you.' The chairs were upright wooden ones and had probably been on the planet longer than Duncan himself.

'The lighthouse service divides into three parts,' he began. 'There are ourselves, the keepers of the light. We are at the coal face, if you like. We won't be there for long mind. They are already talking about automation, but at the moment fog is on our side, as I will explain later. Then the second part is made up of the people who service the lights. There are the supply vessels, *Pharos* and *The Pole Star* who take provisions to the more distant lights. They also take out the engineers. But now we have helicopters too, by Jove. There is a lot of building work going on around the lights with heli-pads being constructed, and more often than not the engineers will arrive by air and the keepers will be relieved by helicopter. Most of them come from Inverness on the East coast.

'Now, the final third of the service is known as 84. That's 84 George Street in Edinburgh where you were interviewed. Och, aye. 84 is the bain of many of our lives. Mostly they don't have a clue. Nice enough people, but city folk. They have their Christmas parties and their golf tournaments, and we all get to read aboot it in the Journal. They live *ordinary* lives,' and the stress Duncan put on the word 'ordinary' only added to the excitement I felt at being on my first light. 'They work from nine to five,' Duncan continued, 'and then they go home to the suburbs. They've never had to kill a sheep or get up to work at two in the morning in storm force winds. They dinnae ken how a light works. Anyway, they tell us that we should be in the light room at all times when we are on watch. But that's plain daft. There are other things to be done about the place. If you stayed up here all night you'd be more likely to fall asleep than if you keep yourself occupied. The crucial thing is to be up here every half an hour to wind the weights and to check on the pressure. If you want to prepare the soup for tomorrow's dinner or watch a bit of television before close down then that is your business. Am I making myself plain? Now, let's step outside and enjoy the view.' At this point I noticed a large door, or hatch, in the side of the lightroom, the sort I'd imagine on a submarine.

'This opens inwards, you'll be glad to know if you ever have to go out here in a gale, as you probably will at some point.' I followed Duncan out to the rim of the light and quickly bonded with the waist-high metal rail. The view was stunning.

Out to the west the sun was setting. The evening was warm. The sea was as flat as a mirror, which I would soon be taught was not just a cliché but a technical term in weather forecasting. Seals. Oyster catchers. Gulls. All settling down for the night.

'What's that?' I asked Duncan, pointing towards a large fin in the water. It looked like a B-movie shark cutting through the water.

'Och, it's only a shark,' Duncan replied in his slow Gaelic lilt. 'A basker. They love this little island. Quite harmless are basking sharks. The only danger you'd be in from one was if you were out rowing and it came up underneath your boat. I've seen them as big as thirty feet. There were aboot six o' them yesterday. A marine biologist who visited once told me they like the warmth of the sea at this time of year, coming up in the Gulf Stream. My own theory is that they think this little island is itself a giant shark and that is why they swim so close to shore. I haven't seen so many off any other lighthouse, and I've served on over twenty. I expect you will fall in love with Pladda, Peter. Everybody does.'

I marvelled at it all. On one side the sea seemed to stretch away forever. On the other the little farmhouses on Arran appeared to be within touching distance. The noises of the city, the traffic and crowds all seemed so far away – but so were the noises of the towns, the villages, the crofts. Here, we had got right down to four men and nature. Or three men, a boy, and a spaniel . . . and a shark.

'Aye, it's a bonnie night, Peter,' Duncan said. 'Almost the longest day of the year. Have you ever been to Orkney? It is a truly magical place so it is. I've served on three lights up there at different times of my career. If we were up there this week the sun would just be tipping under the horizon not long before midnight.'

'Do you always come out here after you've got the light going?' I asked.

'A good question. And it reminds me of everything else I have to teach you.'

In the twilight Duncan reminded me a little of Jack Warner who used to play Dixon of Dock Green, the benign television bobby. Duncan was a big man but had a great gentleness about him.

'The most important time to come out on the rim is at midnight. Whether sleet or hail or storm force winds, every keeper on watch on every lighthouse will be out checking on every other light. It is generally possible to see three or four other lights from your own one. In a minute I will show you the log book where we check them off. It is chust another way of keeping us on our toes. You see, all the other lights that can see you will be checking that your light is still burning at midnight. And you cannae cover up for a friend on another light, because if you say his was burning but two other stations say it was not, well then that is both of you out of a job. The only time lighthouses never burn at night is during war time. I was sent to North Africa during the war,' and a cloud of dark remembrance seemed to pass across this good man's face. 'But the keepers who remained would only light the lights when the British navy were coming in or out. For the rest of the time the lights stayed out. But it is a dirty business, war. I hope you never see it Peter.'

'At least it would be over quickly,' I replied philosophically.

'Well, I would not count on anything in this world. If it is in the interests of the politicians they will find a way to stretch it out. But there is a safe on every lighthouse with instructions on what to do in the event of a nuclear war. Only the Principal Keeper has the key to it. I have never been tempted to look, and I pray to God I never have to. That is why they get us all to sign the Official Secrets Act.'

We both leaned against the rail in silence after that. It was growing dark and I could see other flashes on the horizon, very faint at first, each sending its own signal. Around us our own beam grew in intensity as the light faded. It was getting cooler and I pulled my donkey jacket tight around me. I'd been born into a world where war was still the daily topic of conversation even though it had ended eight years earlier. 'We're all lucky to be alive,' was the message at school, and at home, and in church. And of course we were. Growing up in Glasgow in the fifties was growing up in a heavily bombed city still rebuilding itself. Not as bad as Dresden or Coventry but worse than many others. There had been rationing, and I remember old ration cards in a drawer at home amongst the string and the rubber bands. The Cold War was just beginning to kick in. My parents would listen to *Any Questions* on the radio as I half-listened while playing on the floor. Sober politicians and minor celebrities would field questions about capital punishment and the introduction of parking meters or VAT. Sir Gerald Nabarro would say his piece alongside Enoch Powell and Anthony Wedgewood Benn. But there was always a question about nuclear weapons and the threat from China and the Soviet Union. There never seemed to be an answer. Only a growing anxiety as the nuclear stockpiles increased.

Our nostalgic musings on the rail were interrupted by the need to wind up the weight and check the paraffin pressure. After that, Duncan suggested a cup of tea. The kettle was of course boiling and I had the honour of preparing the pot. At last I felt I was doing something useful.

'Now, before the next winding,' Duncan told me, 'I better tell you how to forecast the weather.' There seemed so much to learn, I thought. I was beginning to feel tired – not from any great physical exertions, but from entering a new universe.

'Have you heard of the Beaufort Scale?' My blank look must have signified a resounding no.

'Well then, let us begin at the beginning. The weather is really a very ordered thing, och, yes,' Duncan continued, and I wondered how many student lighthouse keepers had acquired 'the knowledge' through his lucid teachings.

'Whether you are observing a sea breeze or a thunderstorm you are looking at something that is happening for a reason. Much of what we call weather happens because of the air around us. And it happens because some of the air is cooler and some warmer than the rest. Out of this is born your tropical cyclone and your bracing wind on a frosty morning. But let us start with the sea breeze.'

My only previous weather lesson had been listening to Billy Connolly in one of his earlier incarnations somewhere between the Clyde shipyards and the Hollywood Hills. Then he was one half of a duo called The Humblebums, the other being Gerry Rafferty who went on to record the big hit 'Baker Street'. I once saw them play the City Halls in Glasgow, Connolly hoarsely out of tune but making up for it with wild enthusiasm. I remember the verse: 'It only rains when clouds bang together, but every-body knows that . . .'

That had been about my awareness of the mechanics of met-eorology. Duncan was now upping the ante in a Captain Birdseye sort of way.

'A sea breeze happens when the air above the land is heated by the sun more than the air above the sea.' Duncan's big hands moved like the flapping wings of old dark crows as he described the meeting of different weather fronts. 'The air over the land heats and when it does it expands. This makes a high pressure area about two thousand feet up. This in turn pushes an air flow out to sea. Are you following me?'

To my surprise, I think I was.

'This same air then falls slowly over the sea as it cools. In other words the pressure is rising on the land and descending on the sea and this motion causes the sea breeze to move across the shore.' Duncan took a large mouthful of tea. 'The reason that this is important to us is that all rock and island lighthouses have to send weather reports every few hours to the nearest coastal lighthouse which in our case is Corsewall. I'll show you how to do that later. Sometimes we just check to see that the radio is working, other times we have to send a full weather report, and that is where the Beaufort Scale comes in.' He took a typed piece of paper from the drawer of the sideboard. 'You will find a copy of this up in the light room. Basically it is a scale from zero to twelve. You see it goes from calm through to hurricane, which is the general description of the condition. Then there is a description of it at sea, then on land, followed by the limits of velocity in knots. Just take it slowly and you'll no' get in a fankle.'

I floated in and out of knowingness and unknowingness as Duncan spoke, but slowly it made sense and in an increasingly poetic sort of way.

'Everything is described as it appears at sea and as it appears on land. At sea, "0", or "calm", is described as "Sea like a mirror" while on land "smoke rises vertically". Just try and picture it,' Duncan advised. 'Imagine it in your mind's eye. "1" is "light air" which at sea means "ripples" and on land "Direction of wind shown by smoke drift but not by wind vanes".' Duncan pointed at the typed descriptions and I noticed the irregular registration of the typeface from an old office typewriter. '"2" is "Light breeze", "small wavelets" or "Wind felt on face, leaves rustle", through to "5", "fresh breeze", "Moderate waves, many white horses, chance of some spray," and "7", "Near gale", on land – "Whole trees in motion", velocity 28 to 33.'

This was all much more real than Michael Fish on the BBC with his isometric pressure, occluded fronts and pullovers that looked like they had been knitted by a mad aunt in the attic. Mind you, I thought, from now on I'll be supplying Michael with some of his data. Maybe I should write him a letter and introduce myself.

'Dear Michael, Did you know that one of the first rules of fashion is never to wear checks with stripes?' But Duncan was pulling me back to Zen and the Art of Weather-forecasting.

Beyond Severe gale 9 (chimney pots and slates removed) and Storm force 10 (trees uprooted, considerable structural damage occurs). I noticed that there were no descriptions for Violent Storms (11) and Hurricanes (12).

'So you have to use your eyes, Peter. That's what this job is all about. That and your common sense. Tomorrow I will teach you how to judge the height of clouds. Then the day after that I will show you how to set the calibrations in the fog room. But I think that's enough for one night. It will soon be time to wind the light again.'

It did not take long for me to drop off to sleep, for I knew I would be up again soon.

I lay in my bed thinking about the wind, trying to visualise its different nuances and strengths. I curled up in a tight foetal position, gripping Flann O'Brien's *The Third Policeman*, and drifted towards sleep: 'There are four winds and eight sub-winds, each with its own colour. The wind from the east is a deep purple, from the south a fine shining silver. The north wind is a hard black and the west is amber. People in the old days had the power of perceiving these colours . . .'

Better Than an All-Day-Breakfast

Hell's bells. At least that's what it sounded like. Two ten second rings, that's how Duncan had advised me to wake the others, and that's how someone was now waking me. It was five-thirty in the morning and I hadn't fallen asleep until after midnight. This was worse than being a student. We'd finished our watch at ten. Thirty minutes before that we had roused Ronnie with the same two long rings. He appeared fifteen minutes later in jeans and a sweater, rubbing the sleep from his eyes. It was at this point that I was introduced to that most collegial of lighthouse traditions by which the bed-going keeper prepares the work-going keeper for the duties ahead – mainly making sure he stays awake. It goes something like this.

Tea, biscuits, and cheese had already been prepared. Duncan and I did this before Ronnie appeared. At first, one keeper will be doing the talking and looking forward to bed while the other's heavy lids will gradually lift from their sleep-drugged state to full alertness. Only on Pladda, where I was being trained, did I share these moments of companionship with two other men, and only for a few days because in my second week I would be driving the lighthouse on my own – and from then onwards there would only ever be two of us at these magical changes of watch. On every light I worked, my fellow keepers would have wild tales about their exploits in the army in post-war Hamburg in the Forties, or the gold mines of Western Australia in the Fifties, or of fights on the deck of trawlers in the North Sea in the Sixties when the flash of steel from a fish-gutting knife was followed by a dull thump and the cry of 'man overboard'. Outside our lighthouse the wind and ocean would oblige with the required sound effects.

Some would talk about the wartime dance halls of the Forties, of Vera Lynn and Arthur Askey, the VE Day celebrations and deals done with wide boys and pimps in Blytheswood Square at the back of Sauchiehall Street or down on Leith docks. Those a generation younger would speak of their days of national service. A few fought in Korea. For them, Elvis Presley, the electric guitar and the Marshall amp seemed to come from nowhere, along with television and hotdogs. Then there were a few men who were only ten years older than me. Their early years had been fixed somewhere between Helen Shapiro and The Kinks. They had followed the transition of Cassius Clay into Mohammad Ali. Their holidays were increasingly being taken in Benidorm instead of Butlin's. They had been born during the war and their lives would always be stamped by the immediacy that war brings to the everyday. I was as mesmerised by the stories of all these men (I must have worked with over twenty) as the rabbits and rats outside were by the beam of our lighthouse.

I did not have much to offer in return. I had after all just turned twenty and it was still 1973. Two years earlier I was a schoolboy waiting for my Scottish Higher leaving certificates ('Are you an idiot, boy!? Do you want to spend the rest of your life working in a shoe shop!?' – this being the lowest rung on the middle-class ladder before the great leveller of unemployment started to bite a decade later – 'And get a haircut while you're at it!!! Do not hide your earlobes under a bushel of hair. Get a haircut! Get a haircut!' – this from an amalgam of teachers attempting to survive what had still to be named as their mid-life crises).

I wasn't sure I wanted to go on to further study. Certainly not at university which had always seemed a graveyard for creativity; art school might be different. But hitch-hiking to India seemed more appealing, especially with the escalating war in Vietnam threatening a global apocalypse now rather than later.

At school I had read Kerouac's *On the Road* shortly before he died, and was itching to get on the road myself. So in my examinations I calculatedly, and secretly, aimed at the bare minimum in terms of results. I would let chance take its course. If I failed to get in to art school, as a large part of me hoped I would, then I would take to the open road – Amsterdam, Tangier, Nepal, and maybe on to Australia or South America. If that sounds foolhardy and self-indulgent now, my only apology is that I measured it, as I and my friends measured so many things, against the yardstick of being sent to Vietnam. It was known as the 'domino effect' and it was what would bring Britain into the war, or so our teachers kept telling us; we had dark visions of the jungle training, the shaved heads, the cluster bombs and napalm, the treachery in the Gulf of Tonkin. These were not Hollywood props and backdrops, as they would later become. This was happening, and there was no damn sign of it coming to an end. Teenagers in America, New Zealand, and Australia had for a long time been conscripted, and our Modern Studies teacher was always harping on about 'the domino effect', 'the domino effect', 'the domino effect', 'Get a haircut!', 'Fuck off!'

Through the reverse telescope of youth I did not realise of course that it was a tiny percentage of my generation who were actually being conscripted, and even fewer killed. (But what of the Vietcong?) As far as I was concerned my generation were all there and we should stop the war immediately and bring them back. And stop bombing villagers whose only protection against heavy metal warfare was straw huts and underground tunnels.

My only other excuse is of course that I was a teenager, those self-righteous years free of all responsibility, those years which combine the wisdom of old age with the temper tantrums of the toddler and miss out the dull responsible stuff in-between.

There appears to be a still, fixed point at the heart of everyone's late adolescence – not long after you get over the bizarre waste and inconvenience of hosting an erection every ten minutes of your waking life. Just imagine dear reader, especially if you are a woman, what it is like to feel a snake-like creature expanding in your pants to what feels like the size of a balloon and must surely be noticed by all . . . but I digress, I was talking about that fixed point in adolescence when on the one hand you think you will live forever, when so much is concertinaed into a day let alone a month or a year. Several lifetimes seem possible and the index of possibility just grows and grows, yet on the other hand the nuclear age has brought with it the 'live for the day' mentality. At least that's how it felt for me. The more experience I had of life the more there seemed to be to experience. Perhaps for the first time ever teenagers around the world felt more in common with each other, no matter what country they came from – *Talkin' 'bout my generation* . . . – than they did, ungratefully, with their elders – *Hope I die before I get old . . .'*

But for me all that was about to change. Six months of living with men from several generations showed me that there had once been a teenager in all of us even if I hadn't yet met the old man in me. And Vietnam was not the only war, as my grandfathers could testify, to which you could be sent.

But when I found myself joint caretaker of a lighthouse and it was my turn to go off watch and spin a few yarns to the keeper waking up for duty, I found I didn't really have much to say that would impress an ex-trawlerman or a retired submarine commander. If I'd joined the service now, in my mid-forties as most of them had, then I could have regaled them with a catalogue of personal disasters and sent them chortling up the stairs to wind up the light with a smile on their face. Like the time I was mugged in the Canary Islands; or when I fell off a stage in Melbourne giving a lecture; when I was nearly blown up in the Guildford pub bombings, or trapped in total darkness in a tiny lift in a mock-Tudor hotel in Tahiti on a journey to find the last resting place of Gauguin. But that was all up ahead. In 1973 my store of life's experiences was still pretty low. So I would tell my fellow keepers about life at art school. They generally liked to hear about the nude models in the life class, and the goings-on in the Tavern Bar, the anti-apartheid demonstrations, the discos and the student sit-ins.

'And how's Peter done on his first night?' Ronnie asked Duncan who was pouring the tea for the three of us.

'Och, I think the laddie's learning,' Duncan replied generously. 'It wisnae sae long since you were being trained up if I remember rightly.'

'Duncan was a senior keeper then on Chicken Rock, before Lachlan Fairbairn turned it into what it is today,' Ronnie said, intriguingly. 'He's the devil of a man. My first night on a light was over ten years ago, and it was Duncan on Chicken Rock who trained me up. Taught me all about the tides and how to navigate by the stars.'

'Who's Lachlan Fairbairn?' I asked.

'Och, you will hear quite enough aboot him if you stay in the service more than a few days,' Duncan said. 'Let's not start on Lachlan now or we'll be up all night. A'body's got their favourite Lachlan story.'

And so the banter kept going for almost fifty minutes with Ronnie regretting having missed *The Dick Emery Show* and *Ironside* on account of having to get some sleep before the watch began, and Duncan saying they didn't watch it anyway because Finlay wanted to see the *Single-handed Yacht Race* on BBC2. 'I think 84 should order us some of those video recorders. They're the latest thing in the States,' Ronnie said, more in hope than expectation, although eventually they would come just a little bit before the same advanced technology made lighthouse keepers like him redundant.

'New-fangled stuff, you don't need any of that,' Duncan told him. 'So long as I get Roy Plumley and *Desert Island Discs* on the wireless I am content,' Duncan said.

'Have you no' written in to Roy yet? Told him you're a lighthouse keeper?' Ronnie enthused. 'I keep telling you Duncan, they'd fly you down to London, show you the sights and give you some fine purvey into the bargain.'

Eventually I got to my bed and enjoyed six hours of very deep sleep. I learned this was the longest amount I could ever expect to get, often sleep came in very short but welcome packages of two hours or four hours – day and night. Then – as if suddenly being thrust back on stage into a different scene – I was back in the same living-room-cum kitchen with Duncan and this time Finlay Watchorn who was going off duty at six in the morning, having relieved Ronnie at 2 a.m.

'It's a fine morn', Duncan said, taking a biscuit from the large ceramic plate with green edging that sat next to the stewing tea. The sun was already over the horizon and the sea changing from a fine dark blue to aquamarine. I was still half submerged in oceanic dreams with sharks, dolphins and seals. It is an unforgettable kind of tiredness when your head seems to be the size of a small planet and your consciousness is at its distant centre trying to reach out to the surface. But I would discover how this would inflate to a giant planet, a monstrous planet, when it came time to wake for a 2 a.m. watch after a hard day's work and only four hours' sleep.

Finlay went immediately to his bed as he would get less than two hours of sleep until breakfast – a breakfast that Duncan and I were about to prepare.

The coming of the fridge and the deep freeze had been a great boon to lighthouse keeping as I was frequently told. In the nineteenth century, cows, goats, and chickens, had to be brought out to be slaughtered when fresh meat was not available on the more remote islands. Duncan raided both appliances as if he were preparing for a visit from the Commissioners themselves. A dozen eggs, a whole black pudding, a loaf of bread, a large packet of bacon, a punnet of mushrooms, six tomatoes, eight sausages . . . it just kept coming.

'You set the table, laddie. Finlay's already switched the light off, but if this were earlier or later in the year it would still be burning and we would have to juggle breakfast preparations in-between light duties.' He produced a bowl of lard from the lower shelf of the fridge.

'You'll find everything you need in the two top drawers of the sideboard. We won't need a fire today, but sometimes in summer we do and this is the watch when it would be lit.'

'Will I be on every watch with you, Duncan?' This was something I had been wondering for a while.

'Och, no, we'll switch you round. So we see how you get on with other men and just to get you into the rhythm of the job. I'll be on from ten till two tonight, and before that Finlay will be doing six till ten, but you've already done that watch with me so I think I'll give you to Ronnie who's on duty from two till six in the morning. Just make sure you get a few hours sleep beforehand as you won't get much after.'

As we talked, Duncan cracked eggs and stripped bacon from the packet, handing me any rubbish to put in the bin. 'You might like to look out the cereal packets and the toast rack while I push on with this,' he said. The smell of bread and mushrooms frying in one pan, and eggs and bacon in the other was dizzying. 'I'll need to do the black pudding and sausages separate, there disnae seem to be enough room,' he said, genuinely surprised. 'But we can keep everything hot in the oven.'

I had just finished setting the table when Duncan asked me if I would give the other two keepers 'two bells each' and call them up for the first meal of the day.

My bell ringing called Finlay and Ronnie in to breakfast and soon we were eating and planning the day ahead.

'Did I tell you 84 want us to build a road down to the jetty?' Duncan mused over a forkful of black pudding.

'A fucking road next?' Finlay exclaimed in genuine surprise. 'I thought they wanted us to rebuild the jetty.'

'Aye, that too,' Duncan replied, 'and watch your language.'

'A fucking road!' Finlay was obviously astonished. 'They're mad, I tell you, mad. There's no' a lot of traffic round these parts after all.'

'It'll be for the tractor,' Ronnie said decisively. 'We're aye having to get replacement parts – replacement tractors – it's that bumpy down to the jetty.'

'Well, whitever,' Duncan continued, buttering some toast. 'We won't be doing it today, or the morn's morn if it comes to that. They tell me the sand and the bitumen will be arriving on the Saturday relief when me and Ronnie go ashore.'

'Oh, I see,' Finlay countered. 'Nice timing or what? So me and the laddie and Stretch will have to do it.'

'And the Professor, he'll be here too, don't forget,' said Duncan. 'The laddie's still on training so you'll have four pairs of hands on deck.'

I don't know whether I was more intrigued by the thought of who might belong to the names 'Stretch' and 'the Professor', or more annoyed at Captain Birdseye calling me laddie all the time.

'So what have we got to look forward to today, big man?' Ronnie asked Duncan.

'I think we'll make a start on painting the exterior woodwork, seeing as how we've got an art student with us,' Duncan winked at me. 'The paint's been sitting there for months and the weather should stay dry for a few days. You can do the window frames, the boy can do the doors, and I'll tackle the fence. Whoever finishes first can help the others.' Less of this 'boy' business, I thought to myself.

'And I'll be in here making lunch,' Finlay said. 'Steak-and-kidney pie today with baked Alaska pudding for afters. A tricky bugger to make but well worth the effort.'

'If you say so, Finlay,' Duncan intoned. 'Now let's get these dishes washed.'

Summer of the Creep

'It's not such a bad life, being a lighthouse keeper,' Finlay addressed me across the dinner table while Duncan and Ronnie nodded in agreement. 'We work a month on and a month off, plus we get our annual holidays so that brings us down to less than six months on the lighthouse in every year. Mind you, we're supposed to stay close to home during our month off. Officially we are still on duty, but there's not much to do besides cutting the grass of the keepers' houses. Would you care for some more steak and kidney, Peter?'

'We all get a free house,' Ronnie took up the story. 'Often there's a street of houses on the mainland, like in Oban, and all the lighthouse keepers and their families who work on the lights in that area will live in the same street. The wives all get to know each other and there's always a few keepers about who are on their month off.'

'We may not get paid a fortune, but there's no' a lot to spend it on,' Finlay said, shovelling some more roast potatoes onto Duncan's plate. 'Over the years you move from house to house and coast to coast. There's a furniture allowance and a school uniform allowance since that changes as often as the family home.

Mind you, the bairns would be growing up anyway and need new clothes, but it's all welcome. Some put money by to purchase a house when they retire.'

'But 84 are now telling us that with automation it may be possible to stay on rent free in lighthouse accommodation after we retire,' Duncan said. 'And in my case that's not so far away. They've made it known they'd also be happy for anyone to retire to an island and live next to the light itself. That way they get a free keeper on site once the light's been automated.'

'Willnae suit our Ronnie, though,' Finlay joked. 'He'll be back to the dark valleys of Perthshire and his mushroom farming.'

'And you'll doubtless be sailing your chicken coop up the Clyde. Has Captain Watchorn told you about his pride and joy?' Ronnie asked me.

'Finlay here is building himself a wee boat behind the vegetable garden,' Duncan explained. 'If you go round the back of the shed you'll see it. He's been at it for over two years, but we all need a hobby on the lighthouses, is that not right, Mr Noah?'

'Don't you listen to them, Peter,' Finlay said. 'You're most welcome to come and inspect her any time you want. All she needs now is a lick of paint and we'll have her launched next week with a bit of luck.'

We'd spent the morning painting the windows and doors bottle green and I had worked up a fine appetite. As Finlay cleared up the meat plates and produced his promised baked Alaska pudding from the oven, Ronnie and Duncan returned to the evergreen topic of automation.

'At the moment we've got fog on our side,' Duncan explained. 'The scientists in their laboratories have not yet come up with a way of detecting fog as accurately as the human eye can do it. So what they are planning to do in the first phase of automation is to keep at least one lighthouse in every area fully manned.

That way the keepers on those lights can automatically turn on the fog signal on the others, when necessary. But I'm sure it will no' be long until in their wisdom they solve that problem too and our jobs will be totally redundant.'

'To be sure, the Pterodactyl will be the last lighthouse keeper,' Ronnie said cryptically.

'Who on earth's the Pterodactyl?' I wondered aloud.

'That's just Ronnie's not inaccurate nickname for the Lighthouse Board's roaming engineer,' Duncan explained in his now familiar soft Hebridean lilt. 'He comes out of the sky in his helicopter and is a man of very strange habits. He is lanky and thin, with very little flesh on his bones, and if you ever see him eating at table, as I'm sure you will if you last out the summer, you will doubtless see a striking similarity to the extinct prehistoric bird.'

'But we're the ones who'll be extinct,' Finlay butted in, dishing up the pudding. 'I reckon I'll be out of a job in the next ten years the way things are going. And I'll still be in my fifties. Who's going to give me another job at that age? What will I do?'

'You can mess about in your little chicken coop,' Ronnie joked. 'You might get a job as an island postman round the Kyles of Bute.'

'Well, may God forgive them for what they are about to do to our jobs,' – it was Duncan now, anger in his voice – 'for I will find it very difficult in my own heart to forgive them. There have been lighthouses for thousands of years, and you only need speak to a sailor or a seaman to know that the human presence is as welcoming as the light itself.'

'Not that we have ever been allowed to go out and rescue someone from a shipwreck,' Ronnie said, and I was surprised.

'Our first duty is to the light,' Duncan explained. 'If a fishing boat or a yacht were to crash into a nearby rock or skerry we can radio through Corsewall to the lifeguards but we are not supposed to make a rescue ourselves.'

'Why not?' I asked.

'Well, think it through laddie. If one of us went out and got into difficulty ourselves and then the other two went out to help there would be no one left to man the light. It might be two in the morning and if we were all drowned trying to rescue a few lost souls the light would soon go out and dozens more lives would be put at risk.'

'May I say this is a very fine baked Alaska pudding, Captain Watchorn,' Ronnie broke in. 'But can we get the dishes done now? *Emmerdale Farm* will be on in twenty minutes.'

'Och, you and your television,' Duncan muttered. 'Where will it all end?'

Ronnie warmed up the television set while we washed and dried a small mountain of plates, pots and pans.

Suddenly we were transported across the world again to Washington and the Watergate hearings. Ronnie, of course, had been following the historic unfolding of events as closely as any of his daily soap operas. Jeb Stuart Magruder, deputy director of CREEP, the aptly named Campaign to Re-elect the President, was about to re-take the stage. Attorney General John Mitchell was waiting in the wings.

'Old Jeb put the finger on John Dean the other day,' Ronnie explained. 'It was better than Perry Mason so it was.'

'They say that Mitchell's wife's a bit of a lush,' Finlay added, obviously he'd been following events as closely as Ronnie. 'I wonder what her tipple is?'

'Probably Bacardi and Coke,' Ronnie ventured authoritatively. 'That's a good pool-side drink and I rather fancy she takes the odd break in the Caribbean, what d'you think, Peter?'

I was totally enthralled. Magruder was spilling the beans about an 'espionage plan' hatched by J. Gordon Liddy which apparently involved high-class call girls and a yacht anchored off Miami.

'Nice work if you can get it,' Finlay commented.

'They will all burn in Hell,' Duncan decreed, and disappeared to his room.

Meanwhile, Magruder was describing one of Liddy's loopier schemes. It involved kidnapping radical political leaders and holding them in Mexico until after the Republican National Convention, thus stopping any unwanted demonstrations against Nixon. Then the bombshell. Funds would also be made available to set up a private brothel in Miami for the convention.

'It gets better and better,' said Finlay, rubbing his hands with glee and looking even more than usual like Captain Haddock. He pushed his cap back on his head and bit the end of his pipe.

Someone called Senator Weicker was now in the inquisitorial chair.

'Did Mr Haldeman know perjury was going to be committed at the trial of the Watergate burglars?' he asked Magruder.

'Yes, I think that would be correct,' replied the deputy chief of CREEP, slipping a Life Saver under his tongue. Soon the debate honed in on the matter of some $5000 found on the Watergate burglars, and just as the argument was growing more focussed, Ronnie, with a cry of alarm, drew our attention to the fact that *Emmerdale Farm* had already started on the other channel and we reluctantly bade Washington farewell for another day.

That night I went to bed at eight o' clock and desperately wished myself to sleep. In a little over five hours I would be starting my first 2 a.m. watch and I wanted as much rest as possible.

Ronnie was my companion on this particular 'Rembrandt', and we were both woken on cue by Duncan. I can still remember how difficult it was getting out of bed that first time. It was cold and it was dark and against all forecasts (our own, presumably) there was rain drumming against the small window of my bedroom.

'Give the laddie a cup of tea,' Duncan instructed Ronnie, 'and I'll leave the two of you to it, you can keep each other awake and I'm ready for my bed.'

'So are you enjoying yourself? Being a lighthouse keeper I mean,' Ronnie asked me after Duncan had gone.

'Very much,' I replied honestly. 'I just hope I do the job properly.'

'I think you'll be fine, and Duncan will write you a good report,' he added ominously.

'What sort of a report?'

'All you students get two weeks training and the PLK has to send a report on your progress and suitability to 84. By no means everyone gets through their training, but I can tell Duncan is pleased with the way you are going. Now we better get up and wind that light.'

We spent most of the watch up in the light chamber or leaning against the rail when the rainy squall subsided. Ronnie told me about his hobbies which in addition to interacting with the television set included practising his golf swing when he was on the lighthouse and playing it for real when he went ashore. Comet the spaniel, as I later witnessed, was always keen to join in – fetching the practice ball and bringing it back to Ronnie's tee.

'What will you do when automation comes?' I asked him.

'If it happens sooner rather than later I'll try and get myself another job. If later rather than sooner I always had a mind to travel, see a bit of the world. A lot of keepers sort of retired into this job after living and working all over the world. I sort of came into it earlier than most, which means I should get promoted to PLK younger than most.'

'How's that?' I asked.

'Well it's the old thing of dead men's shoes. Promotion comes strictly through length of service. There's no real way, or fair way, to monitor a keeper's progress, and you can't expect your fellow keepers to do it, so it all goes by length of service. That's why even the Lachlan Fairbairns of this world eventually become PLKs.'

There was that name again. 'Who is this Lachlan Fairbairn?' I asked. We were leaning on the rail as the white light cut through the blackness that surrounded us. Below, waves crashed on invisible rocks.

'Everybody has their Lachlan stories,' Ronnie began. 'I suppose he's the only real eccentric that 84 tolerates in the service and he's been a keeper longer than most. Due to retire next year they tell me. I worked with him on Inchkeith and Chicken Rock. That's when he became PLK, on the Chicken, and they've left him there ever since while other keepers move onwards and upwards.'

'So why's he eccentric?' The wind blowing hard against my cheeks, my fingers turning numb inside the pockets of my donkey jacket.

'Well, for starters, soon as he arrives on a light, the first thing he does is take all his clothes off. Spends the whole month buff naked. It's a frightening sight, especially if he's frying sausages. Then there is his one-stringed fiddle, like an off-its-heid sort of violin with a gramophone horn attached to one end. It makes the most eerie sounds.'

I held my silence the better to keep Ronnie talking.

'When I worked with him on Inchkeith his current hobby was making clothes pegs, like the kind gypsies make. You get a couple of wee bits of wood and hold them together with a ring pull from a beer can. Lachlan used to spend all his spare time in one of the out-houses, whittling wood and assembling these clothes pegs. I remember one year the Commissioners made their annual visit,' Ronnie was laughing so much he could hardly speak, 'and there was Lachlan, stark-naked, sitting in the dining room with a chocolate box full of pegs. "Does your wife wash?" he asked the head Commissioner, and taken aback the poor man said "Yes, of course." "Then give her these," and Lachlan presented him with the Milk Tray box. "Tell her they're my best ones, mind, and she'll have to pay next time if she wants more." He ranked them depending on how good he thought the beer was that the ring-pull came from. Then without missing a beat he produced his one-stringed fiddle and turning to another Commissioner asked "What's your favourite hymn?" The poor fellow mumbled something about "Rock of Ages" and Lachlan gave us a full five minutes on his fiddle. Sounded a bit like a guy I once heard at the King's Theatre in Glasgow playing a saw. God it was funny.'

Later in the watch I felt I would buckle under the tiredness as the hour changed from four to five. Ronnie kept me talking about student life in Dundee and all my crazy plans for the future. He listened patiently and occasionally took me out on the balcony to blow away the cobwebs.

'You'll have to do this on your own soon. Keep your mind active,' he advised. 'If you feel yourself dozing off, get outside in the wind or splash some cold water on your face. If you really feel you can't hack it then wake someone up. We've all been there ourselves. No one minds being woken.'

We were standing on the rim of the light when the dawn finally began to break. We were both silent, staring into the blackness when between the strobes of the light a thin line of lesser darkness appeared and proclaimed itself to be the horizon. The division became more acute as the tonal contrast increased. It was like watching a Mark Rothko painting take form before our eyes. A slash of pink followed by a band of gold above the horizon and an inky blue below.

'It's light enough to walk down to the jetty,' Ronnie announced. 'If we wind the light just now we'll be back in twenty minutes. It'll do us good to stretch our legs. I'll give Comet a hoy in case he wants to join us.'

And as we descended the steep slope to the sea, Ronnie talked about the different lights he'd worked on.

'Skerryvore's a bugger,' he said. 'Almost straight out the sea, and you're cooped up in the tower for most of your spell of duty. The beds are like coffins, with sides on them, and they are one on top of the other like bunk beds. The weight gets winched up through the floor of your bedroom and up through the ceiling, every half hour. I had to be taken to hospital by helicopter once when I knocked myself out. I must have been having a nightmare and I sat bolt upright and knocked myself out on the bed above me. It wasn't till I didn't show up for my watch that they realised what had happened. Then there was a keeper I worked with there who used to climb down the tower every night and stand on this little patch of rock and shout "Hello!" into the darkness. He claimed it kept him sane, but he got the fright of his life when one night someone shouted "Hello" back. It was a stray yachtsman who thankfully managed to skirt the rock without damage.'

'We got a poem at school about the Flannan Isles and the three lighthouse keepers who disappeared.' I said, wanting to contribute something as we walked carefully down the clover-lined path that was lit every few seconds by our very own lighthouse.

'Aye, I've worked on the Flannans. Every keeper has their own Flannan tales like they have their Lachlan Fairbairn stories. And *Blue Peter* often re-tells it. That Valerie Singleton is some woman. Do you watch it yourself? It's always that John Noakes who gets sent up a lighthouse at Christmas with the tree, or has to climb a chimney stack in Derbyshire. Wee Shep the dog waiting patiently for his return. Grand stuff.'

It was in December 1900 that three lighthouse keepers disappeared without trace from Eilean Mor, one of the Seven Hunters better known as the Flannan Isles. The story goes that when the light went out and the rescue crew arrived they found the dining-room table set for a meal but not a human soul anywhere on the island. The poem was written by Wilfred Gibson. I once saw an opera at the Edinburgh Festival based on the same story, composed by Sir Peter Maxwell Davies who lives on one of the remote Orkney Islands.

The drama of the Flannan Isle begins:

> Though three men dwell on Flannan Isle
> To keep the lamp alight,
> As we steered under the lee we caught
> No glimmer through the night.

and ends

> We thought how ill-chance came to all
> Who kept the Flannan Light,
> And how the rock had been the death
> Of many a likely lad –
> How six had come to a sudden end
> And three had gone stark mad,
> And one, whom we'd all known as friend,
> Had leapt from the lantern one still night
> And fallen dead by the lighthouse wall –
> And long we thought
> On the three we sought,

And on what might yet befall.

Like curs a glance has brought to heel
We listened, flinching there,
And looked and looked on the untouched meal
And the overtoppled chair.

We seemed to stand for an endless while,
Though still no word was said,
Three men alive on Flannan Isle
Who thought on three men dead.

Morning had, as they say, broken. Ronnie and I returned to the
light after sitting down by the jetty where we skimmed pebbles
across the millpond sea. The colony of seals were stretching and
clearing their throats on the other side of the island. It looked
like it was going to be a glorious day. Ronnie gave me his theo-
ries about the Flannan Isles mystery. He said he knew from experience an undercurrent of water could appear from nowhere
even on a flat calm day and push a wall of water high in the air.
One of the keepers might have been fishing and been swept away.
The other two, on going to rescue him met the same fate themselves. 'Contrariwise,' he went on, 'they might have been going a
bit stir crazy and jumped aboard a French vessel. There were a
lot of French ships laden with fine wines and perfumes that came
by the Flannans via a port call in Leith. They'd head round the
top of Scotland and then back down to Brittany.' I didn't know
whether he was pulling my leg or not, so I merely threw another
stone for Comet to chase and rolled a cigarette.

For the past quarter century I have kept in touch with my old
lighthouse colleagues by reading *The Northern Lighthouse Journal*,

the quarterly publication produced by The Northern Lighthouse Board. It has accompanied me to places as far flung as Ulan Bator in Outer Mongolia, Las Vegas and Bangkok. I have settled down by a railway track or the side of a hotel swimming pool and caught up with daily life on the Scottish lights or, more recently, as automation spread, life at 84 George Street.

A series of letters from keepers on the subject of the Flannan Isles has been running for some time and from personal experience J. A. Ross of Inverness sides with Ronnie's first theory. His letter begins:

I was pleased to see in the Christmas number of the Lighthouse Journal the three letters relating to the disaster at the Flannan Islands in 1900.

The following incident which happened to Kenny MacGillivray, Callum McIver and myself could have been what happened in December 1900.

It was a normal day on the Rock. The morning's work had been completed, dinner over and kitchen tidied up. It was then the custom for the Keepers to go for a walk. It was standard practice that there was always to be at least two keepers out together. The other man usually came along, or if he was on the early watch had the choice of going to bed for two or three hours. This day we all decided to go out.

The wind was fresh to strong from the South West but had been blowing from that direction and strength for the past fortnight. On the Flannans one should always remember that the run of the sea under these conditions might have been coming from as far away as South Georgia. There was a heavy sea running and lots of spray so it was a case of oilskins and sea boots. We set out to see if the crane on the West landing was OK. I was walking on the right side of the bogey track, Callum was in the middle and

Kenny on the left. When we were abreast of the first of the four upright posts nearest to the Station a wall of water appeared in front of us. I grasped the post and if I remember rightly Callum grasped a hold of me. I could feel the pull of the sea as it ran back down the cliff. It was only for seconds that we were under the water but when we got the water out of our eyes there was no Kenny. Going to look for him we found him climbing the rock face on his hands and knees. Going and helping him up, we got away from there as quickly as possible. Kenny had been washed down the cliff, and had been stopped from going right over by this large rock to the left of the bogey track. This is the same rock I think referred to in Mr Muirhead's report. The height above sea level when the sea struck us would have been another 60 or 70 feet above that as reported by Mr Muirhead – that is 170 or 180 feet above sea level.

Apart from some bruises and soaked to the skin, which applied to Kenny only, we were unharmed. The same kind of accident could have happened to the Keepers in 1900. Two keepers going for a walk, one could have been injured and the other keeper had gone for help, namely the Occasional Keeper. Mr Moore's letter said that he concluded that Mr McArthur had gone out in his shirt sleeves. Anyone going out dressed like that in these conditions in the middle of December must have done so in dire urgency. When the two keepers got to the injured man another sea could have taken them all away. That is only my suggestion, and after the experience that we had I'll go along with Mr Muirhead's report that the sea was responsible for their deaths.

If these letters regarding the loss of the keepers in 1900 had been made public at the time, it would have prevented lots of surmises by keepers and would have prevented a lot of rubbish being said by outsiders.

The poem about the Keepers at Flannan Island might not have

included the part about the three large black birds that were
supposed to have flown away when the relief party arrived.'

We mused about these and other mysteries as we walked back
up from the jetty to the light. Its beams were almost invisible in
the daylight that had flooded the landscape.

Ronnie now showed me how to turn off the light, going
through the reverse procedure Duncan had shown me on my
first night. We finished by carefully pulling down the blinds and
returning the canister of paraffin to the fog room. It was time to
waken Finlay. I looked at my watch. It was 5.45 in the morning.
We would have a banter with Finlay until 6.15, go to our beds,
and then we'd be up again for breakfast at 8.15. I'd never felt so
tired before. Never. In my head the lyrics from The Velvet
Underground's 'Venus in Furs' lulled me to sleep:

> I am tired, I am weary,
> I could sleep for a thousand years,
> A thousands dreams . . .

Cooking Up a Storm

The only anxiety to darken the idyllic landscape of my first days as a lighthouse keeper was the knowledge that very soon I would have to start cooking.

I had brought with me a thin volume called *Cooking in a Bedsit* which my mother had given me at the start of my student days. I soon realised that merely multiplying everything by four was not going to satisfy my fellow keepers. They required more than student snacks. So, whenever possible, I watched their preparations and furtively made notes in my little yellow notebook.

Soup appeared to be big on Pladda. On a shelf above the sink were rows and rows of sweetie jars filled with pulses and beans of all kinds, some soaking in water for immediate use. There were lentils and dried peas, red kidney beans and haricots, butter-beans and dried prunes, all neatly labelled in a cursive script. A bit like a Damien Hirst installation twenty years before its time.

It turned out that Finlay Watchorn was the great soup *aficionado*. On my third free afternoon I shadowed him in the kitchen and learned what I could.

'You ask an awfie lot o' questions,' he complained eventually.

'Comes o' being a student I suppose. We used to get hit at school if we asked questions, so of course we all shut up and never learned onything.'

I'd already won from him the finer differences between making fish stock and chicken stock and quickly progressed to methods for clarifying butter.

When I joined him he was in the middle of preparing two batches of soup. One was a chicken, bacon, and lentil concoction which he was going to divide up in freezer bags and squirrel away for the long winter nights. The other would be eaten that evening and would use up the crabs which had been caught earlier in the week. To my amazement he showed me the remaining four crabs were still alive and having a 'square go' at each other in a large bucket outside the back door. A couple of sea urchins sat quietly at the bottom of the pail next to a scarlet limpet.

'What we need's a big pan of boiling water. Can you fix that up for me, Peter? Just use what's already boiling in the big kettle,' Finlay said. 'While we're bringing it back to the boil I'll show you how to make a bouquet garni.'

'A book of what?' I asked, not quite catching the strange mix of Celtic-French.

Finlay was wearing his Greek fisherman's cap and pushed it to the back of his head to wipe his brow with a large gingham handkerchief. 'A garni,' he abbreviated. 'It's a fine and dandy way of flavouring soups.' He pulled a few separate ingredients from the vegetable rack and a ball of twine from the kitchen drawer.

'It's awfie easy to make and it gives off a fine aroma. You take a leak, a bayleaf and a sprig of thyme – just like that, as Tommy Cooper would say, – not like that, like that,' Finlay mimicked the hand movements, the famous shrug of the shoulders. 'Now, rummage around for some celery leaves, which I think we've got there, and a wee dod of parsley. Cut a length of string, and hey presto Bob's your auntie. Leave a wee bit tail for easy removal from the pot. Barry Magic!' And with a final flourish he whipped off his cap and there sitting on his head was one of the four remaining crabs. I've no idea how he did it.

'Now we'll just drop this fellow in the boiling water and throw in his cousins for company. Always pick a live crab up from its arse end, that way you keep its claws away from your own.' The more I got to know Finlay the more I felt he should have his own TV programme. Maybe even a cookery show. It would make a welcome change from the starched stuffiness of Fanny Craddock and her zomboid husband Johnnie which Ronnie was always watching.

'We dinnae need to leave them boiling o'er long,' Finlay said. 'Just long enough to make a quick radio check. Come with me,' and I followed him across the forecourt to the base of the tower where all the radio equipment was kept in an adjoining room. This was something else I would have to learn. I took my yellow notebook with me and as I have it in front of me now, a quarter of a century later I can tell you what I wrote:

1) *Radio Room – VHF*
When Bell rings lift receiver, press button on wall then press trigger on receiver. Keep it pressed.
2) *Short Range: Switch on wall receiver the same as above.*
3) *Standard Message:*
'Hello Corsewall, this is Pladda replying. Receiving you loud and clear. No messages for you. All well. Pladda out.'

'Now that's just the standard radio check,' Finlay told me. 'We do that every other watch. But once a day we make a more detailed weather report which ends up down at the BBC. It must be a real bugger's muddle down there with reports coming in frae coastal stations all aroon' the country. They piece it together like a giant jigsaw puzzle. I reckon the met office of the BBC is tae weather forecasting what 84 is tae lightkeeping. Sometimes I think they'd be better throwing their charts away and just looking oot the windae. Probably get it right more often. Has Duncan taught you how to guess the height of clouds yet with his old Gaelic voodoo? Once he's done that he'll let you into the secret of judging the distance of approaching fog. The Zen Calvinists are the boys for that – a steady hand and a sober mind. Comes of being brought up in the Wee Free – nae Christmas presents and nae organ music. All the fun they got as bairns wis looking at clouds and fog. Did you know it is the only religion started by a guy with a speech impediment? "We Free Kings of Orient are . . ." But dinnae tell Duncan. Now, let's get back and see how those crabs are doing.'

Back in the living area Ronnie was watching *Crossroads* and Duncan was absorbed in a copy of *Life and Work*. Finlay and I headed straight for the kitchen.

While the crabs were cooling on the draining board, Finlay assembled everything else he would need to make his crab soup. 'I call it The Devil's Broth on account of the chillies and red peppers that go into it. Nae too much mind or you lose the flavour of the crab a'tegether.'

From a small compartment in the sideboard, which I noticed had his name drawn on it above a skull and crossbones and the warning 'Keep Out – Finlay's Special Purvey', he produced a clutch of exotic ingredients: rice vermicelli, dark soy sauce, a packet of noodles, Thai fish sauce, a small jar of peanut butter . . .

'Now, before I show you how to take a crab apart, we've just enough time to go into the garden and pick the rest o' what we need.' Duncan and Ronnie remained absorbed in their pleasures as we hurtled outside again in search of some raw ingredients. Beyond the small, tidy lawn, yet within the white-walled enclosure of the lighthouse grounds there was a small but impressive vegetable and herb garden. 'Have you seen ma bonnie lassie yet?' Finlay asked me, and I hadn't a clue what he was talking about. 'Ma boat, son. The one I'm building – it's jist doon there beside the foghorn.' And when I looked I could see a little shed with the hull of a boat of some kind protruding from the door. 'Ah hope to launch her next week. She's a wee beauty. The lighthouse wives will be coming across for the ceremony. Three years work on her – but you've gotta have a hobby on a lighthouse. Wait till you meet Stretch next week. Being a difficult bastard's his hobby. He's what you'd call a hardman if he were from Glasgow, but he's frae Aberdeen ken – Furryboot City. Och, well never mind,' as I obviously failed to get his joke. 'He used to be a deep sea fisherman. Have you got a hobby, Peter? I suppose you artists are doing your own hobby all the time. I dunno, getting grants for drawing naked women. Now, this is our little veggie patch. It's Ronnie who's the great gardener, but we all take a turn,' Finlay said. 'Ronnie seems able to grow anything here – mair varieties of tattie than you'll find in yon Findhorn settlement up the east coast. Comes o' growing up in Perthshire I suppose. Now a' we need is a cabbage an' a couple of carrots,' and with a deft twist he yanked them from the sandy soil.

'How did he get the name Stretch?' I asked, and had been dying to since I first heard his name mentioned.

'God knows,' Finlay shuddered. 'I hate to think. A'body's too feart to ask him. And you'll know why when you meet him.'

Over the next half hour he showed me how to separate the sweet white flesh of the crabs from their armour-plating. Up close they looked more menacing than anything NATO could dream up. 'You've got to break the legs at the joints,' Finlay explained. 'Pretend you're a Provo. Then you crack their shells with the handle of your knife. Gie it a really hard smack.'

Gradually a bucket filled up with the discarded outer casing of the crabs while a small dinner plate held a much more modest amount of white meat. 'In some parts of the country they call these the "dead men's fingers",' he explained, pulling at the feathery gills at the side of the crab he was working on. 'Nae use to man nor beast. Just throw them awa.'

With the exception of Duncan who remained true to his Hebridean roots I had trouble recognising the accents of Finlay and Ronnie. It was not until I'd served on other lights and met many more keepers that I realised they all spoke a strange Scottish patois. This was due to the fact that they had all worked – sometimes over decades – all over the country, from the Shetlands to the Borders and across to the Western Isles. On top of that, some like Finlay were great mimics who could drop into the Glaswegian guttural as easily as assuming the quiet Orcadian lilt. Often their tales in the wee small hours would seem studded with a galaxy of dialects. Finlay had a range that included Cockney and Punjabi, but over the crab soup he remained middle-of-the-road Scottish.

'You know how Ronnie there is always watching yon *Blue Peter* kids' programme?' he asked me, for no seemingly apparent reason as he scooped out a leg of crab meat with his darning needle – but loud enough for Ronnie to hear above the banter of *Crossroads*. 'Between you and me I think he's got a crush on yon Valerie Singleton. Has he shown you his *Blue Peter* badges yet?'

'Dinnae you listen to him, Peter, and wheesht the pair o' you. We're at a crucial moment here. Benny's been messing about with Carlos's steak knives and they're going to have to settle it in the car park. Square go. Wait a minute though, here comes Meg, she'll sort them out. You give them what for Meg, dinnae take no nonsense.'

'It's all a lot of nonsense,' Duncan growled from behind his church magazine. 'There is no peace, saith the Lord, unto the wicked.'

'Blimey, I've opened a can of worms here,' Finlay whispered to me. 'Once Duncan starts quoting the bible it can go on as long as the fog signal and be twice as depressing.'

'Comfort ye, comfort ye my people, saith your God. Speak ye comfortably to Jerusalem, and cry unto her, that her warfare is accomplished, that her iniquity is pardoned: for she hath received of the Lord's hand double for all her sins,' Duncan thundered.

'Aye, he's off now,' Finlay gave another stage whisper. 'These Hebrideans hae remarkable memories. Comes o' no' having much else to do that the Lord approves of, save learning his good words by heart and beating your neighbour in their recitation.'

'I heard that Watchorn,' Duncan boomed with some good humour in his voice. 'May ye be forgiven in Heaven as you are damned on Pladda. And if you are ever passing through Stornoway then chust keep passing through.'

'Aye, there's the Zen Calvinist wit coming oot. I thought ye wernae supposed to crack jokes, you Wee Fresians?'

And I thought the first thing Finlay and Ronnie had told me was they didn't make fun of anyone's religion, but this was all good-humoured banter.

'Ecclesiastes Chapter 8 verse 15,' Duncan continued, not batting an eyelid. 'Then I commended mirth, because a man hath no better thing under the sun, than to eat, and to drink, and to be merry: for that shall abide with him of his labour the days of his life which God giveth him under the sun.'

'Disnae sound like the Wee Free I've read aboot,' Finlay observed. 'Now Peter, how did all this begin?'

'Something you were telling me about *Blue Peter*,' I remembered.

'Whit a memory! You sure you're no' really a Zen Calvinist

yoursel'? Whit I was going to say was you ken how Valerie Singleton always has something she prepared earlier so she disnae fuck up on live television like? Well if you pop your head in the fridge you'll find the last of our ingredients under a dish towel on the big platter.'

And there was some kind of white fish already cut into thin strips and lying alongside a dozen mussels and what I later learned was sea urchin flesh.

'Okey-dokey,' Finlay declared. 'Let's get them in the pot. There'll be enough here for the seven of us by the time I've finished.' And he started adding pinches of this and dollops of that to the boiling crab juice which he'd left on the stove.

'What do you mean the seven of us?' I asked.

'Well the four of us here plus Big Tam and his two boys.' I must have looked blank.

'Did Moses here no' tell you we're shearing the sheep tonight?' I continued to look blank.

'Farmer Harris who rowed you across the other day. He'll be coming across with his two farm hands to give his sheep their annual short back and sides. We always lend a hand and provide some soup and bread, for it's hungry work. They may even bring a bottle or two of stout, but that's just between you me and the fencepost. 84 wouldn't want to hear aboot it.'

'Fine by me,' I said, dazed and confused.

I don't know if you've ever been at the business end of a sheep? The first thing to do is to ascertain exactly which end the business end is. Pre-shearing is the hardest when they all look like roadies for Dr Hook. Post-shearing they are more Amen Corner or Slade, with recognisable protruberances.

The field that contained the sheep was small and sloped down to the sea. At the lighthouse end was a double fence through which the sheep were herded, ambushed, shorn and given their half-yearly medication.

If you've ever seen a collie dog working a field of sheep, obeying every whistle, crouching, sprinting, veering with the flock, then that was my role. But I suspect I looked more like an albatross preparing for flight. My arms flailing wildly, my hair caught on the wind. It amused the circling oyster catchers, and Comet barked his approval from the sensible side of the fence.

Once corralled at the top end of the field the professionals stood poised to divert their foe into ever-narrower reaches of the pen. Finlay and I helped hold the sheep in place while two sets of shears gave the equivalent of a number-two razor cut. We soon had them looking like Madison Avenue advertising executives.

Throughout it all the lighthouse keepers worked quietly and efficiently while the farmers shouted instructions and encouragement to each other in broad Scots.

'Och backlie, macbugger'groot 'n shaggit.'

'Patlallie yersel''

'Schematosis Boab mcgrubber.'

'Nae, fuckfelty shitegobber.'

'Aroonaroosi.'

'Cuntapacket tae Skye.'

'Aye, b'Goad.'

'Slanty.'

'Slanty!'

God knows what they were on about. Dialect has always been the Scots secret weapon against the English, but island farmers and Aberdeen fishermen are happy to use it against all-comers, even their own.

'What did you make of that?' Finlay asked me as we formed the advance party back to the kitchen to heat up the soup.

'Couldnae understand a word,' I replied honestly.

'I think they were discussing Watergate, but I cannae be sure. Now, fetch out the loaf and cut some thick slices. I'll get the cheese for those that aren't wanting soup.'

Duncan had remained behind at the lighthouse as he was technically on watch and had to make a radio check. It was still an hour or two before the light needed to be lit.

We all eventually crammed into the little living area. Some sat. Big Tam leaned against the sideboard and uncapped bottles of sweet stout with his belt buckle. They'd brought a crate. Comet chewed a bone.

As the beer mellowed us and the soup warmed us, we eased into each other's accents like feet into increasingly familiar boots. Politics brought us together, got us started. As I remember it, the long-running 'cod war' between Britain and Iceland was discussed from every point of view. Should British frigates be sent? Was fifty miles a fair exclusion zone? Why was Alec Douglas-Hume, known to readers of *Private Eye* as 'Bailie Gaffe', our chief negotiator? Did we really want to lose that badly? Each had their own view on the topic, but most succeeded in being both anti-English and anti-Icelandic in an even-handed sort of way.

Then someone mentioned Skylab. Richard Nixon had been on the lunchtime news chatting by phone to the crew, inviting them back to his ranch at San Clemente on their return from space. Ronnie, who was like some kind of human video tape, then chipped in that four scientists were trapped in a research submarine near Key West and only had enough air for two days. And 'Key West' was the trigger to get Big Tam talking about Humphrey Bogart in his favourite movie. And so the conversation ebbed and flowed in a *film noir* sort of way until one of the farm hands, who turned out to be Big Tam's youngest son, produced a fiddle from out of a battered Adidas sports bag that also contained their shears, and slow tapping his foot against the grate of the fire played a haunting Strathspey that had Duncan hooching and chooching away in the corner as tapping feet spread with the speed of a yawn around the tiny room.

And in the orange haze of unexpected beer and welcome company that had almost doubled our island population to seven human souls and a dog, I tilted my upright chair backwards off the vertical and pondered Scotland, my wholehearted half-nation, twice as proud and four times as stubborn for being cauterised from her former sovereignty. A country of tall thistles leaning this way to Lenin and that to Knox. A country that invented television and was then colonised by it . . . from London by politicians, from America by cartoons, from the near past by film. Duncan excused himself to light the lamp. Finlay topped up our mugs of soup. God it was good! Spicy crab.

My head was spinning, and in the morning, if truth be known, it was a little sore. I'd recently read Noel Coward's 'Notes on an Admiral's Hangover', and took some comfort from the fact that his self-inflicted misery was in an altogether more impressive league than mine. But I'd rather have had a couple of Panadol than a poetry book at that moment.

A Change of Crew

Most aspects of lighthouses – the tower, the living quarters, the gardens, and the routine remained fairly similar, but the human personalities changed dramatically every few weeks. Not so much from good to bad as from strange to wonderful to eccentric. On Pladda, I witnessed just such a change within the space of six days as Duncan and Ronnie and Comet left to be replaced by Stretch and The Professor.

One of the last things Finlay and I had done with our departing colleagues was to clean the lighthouse and its living quarters. Every Saturday morning was devoted to this. It has become something of a cliché that lighthouses are always spick and span, polished brass perfectly reflecting the dust free environment around it. Like most clichés it's founded in truth.

During our free afternoons we would perform our own personal tasks – washing our laundry, drying it on the line in the garden, keeping our bedrooms clean and aired. But on the Saturday we would tackle the bigger jobs – dusting the bookcases, sideboard, and the grandfather clock; brushing out the living quarters and mopping the floors; applying Ajax and elbow grease to the bathroom fixtures and the kitchen sink; checking the food supplies in the freezer room. Then it was on to the light. On that first Saturday, the day of the relief, I was given the job of brushing the steps of the lighthouse from top to bottom while Ronnie took a handful of rags and a tin of Brasso up into the light chamber. Duncan was cleaning the windows down below with old newspapers and paraffin while Finlay started preparing lunch in the kitchen. What amazed me was the good humour with which it was all done. There was always time for a chat or an anecdote, and several times we stopped for tea and biscuits. We could probably have got through these chores with greater speed and efficiency. But there was no rush – there never is on a lighthouse. By late morning everything was spotless and ready for inspection should The Commissioners decide to make one of their surprise visits, for which they were legendary.

Ronnie filled me in on this when I was sweeping down the stairs and he was cleaning the brasswork. The light and her reflectors sat above us like a giant diamond.

'They call them unscheduled visits, but there's not really much of an element of surprise about them – even when they all arrive in a Sea King. Word spreads quickly. I mean they wouldn't travel all the way to Pladda without doing Corsewall and Craigie and Lamlash and so on, so we'd hear about it pretty quickly. Even if they did us first we'd see them coming. And I've never seen a lighthouse look less than 100% anyway. Except on Chicken Rock.'

In my one week as a lighthouse keeper, during which each day seemed to represent a year's learning and maturing for me, I had come to immediately link the words Chicken Rock with Lachlan Fairbairn and to anticipate a good story. I rested my broom against the wall of the tower as Ronnie sat down on the top step.

'You see Lachlan prided himself in not lifting a finger to do anything around the light. The keepers posted to work with him

– and there was a pretty quick turnover – soon gave up trying to do his share of the work as well as their own. It just annoyed him with the result that things would look even worse for the annual visit. The brass was filthy. The light chamber was filled with wood peelings from where he'd sit whittling away at his clothes pegs. He used to pish into the reserve generator when most decent keepers, as you know, would do it over the balcony. It is a mystery throughout the service why he was never sacked. There is a story that it brings good luck to all the other light-houses to have one that is constantly in bad repair, but I think that is a story started by Lachlan himself. Anyway, one year the Commissioners made their scheduled visit to the Chicken, so Lachlan knew well in advance that they were coming. The story I heard from Sandy Crawford, who is now on Rattray Head but who I was then working with on Fair Isle South, is that the Commissioners were taken aback by how much the place had deteriorated since their last visit. And on that previous visit they had threatened to put him on some kind of suspension, although it never happened of course. Anyway, one of the Commissioners said to him that he'd really have to do some-thing with the brasswork, it was in a shocking state. "Nae fear," the wee man replied. "You will not recognise it when you return." And him standing there buff naked by all accounts. The only part of him covered being the top of his chest on account of his long ginger beard.

'Anyway, Peter, they didn't recognise it the following year,' Ronnie laughing near to crying. 'He'd painted every bit of brass bright red. Bright fucking red. All up in the light chamber, the handrail down the stairs, all the brasswork on the fog signal as red as a fire engine and him standing there proud as punch with a big smile on his face. They were speechless, so they were.'

* * *

'So you're off on your summer hols?' Finlay remarked to Ronnie over our last lunch together as a group.

'That'll be the gowlfing,' Duncan replied. 'The devil's favourite pastime.'

'Surely thae dinnae have golf courses in Perthshire?' Finlay continued before Ronnie could reply, his mouth being full of roast chicken and assorted vegetables. 'Far too damp for that. The course would be water-logged the whole time. Water-polo perhaps.'

'But I thocht our man was going over yonder?'

'Whit, like in a séance?'

'Naw, naw, over to the continent,' Duncan replied, as if that was far enough.

'I'm going to Benidorm,' Ronnie finally managed. 'And Comet's off to his favourite kennels.' He tossed the dog a roast potato and the wee fellow was up in the air like Bobby Charlton.

'Heid the ba'! Heid the ba'!' Finlay cried, but Comet just clamped his teeth around it and swallowed hard. Time to go and bark at the seals, and he trotted out of the open front door.

Sharing the island with an assortment of animals, birds, and sea creatures had been one of the many high points of the past week. When I wasn't with my fellow keepers or tending the light I would clamber down the rocks to the shore and just sit quietly, watching, thinking, rolling cigarettes and pondering just when I would finally give up smoking. A dark nicotine cloud was the only one in the otherwise blue skies of my life around 1973. I didn't like to admit that I was addicted, but I was. Increasingly I got less pleasure from each cigarette I smoked, and increasingly I needed another one.

Dying of cancer wasn't the worry. I was pretty sure none of my generation would live long enough for that to happen – not with the way Vietnam was heading. But my sense of taste and smell were going too, and besides, it was a waste of money that could otherwise be spent replenishing my record collection. I hadn't bought a new Pink Floyd since *Ummagumma*, and as for Leonard Cohen I badly wanted another copy of *Songs from a Room* as my original was so scratched from constant late-night play.

So, with my cigarette, I would sit in this favourite spot amongst the rocks of Pladda and watch the basking sharks slowly circle the island. They were beautiful creatures. Quite hypnotic in their movements. At one point between wanting to be an astronaut and wanting to go to art school I had planned to be a marine biologist. With hindsight it was really the colours of the tropical fish and the coral reef that excited me.

My father is a zoologist and as a child I kept as wide a range of pets as you could imagine: hedgehogs, grass snakes, lizards, rabbits, tropical finches, plus the standard cat, dog and guinea pig. Well before going to primary school at the age of five I was familiar with the inner workings of the zoology department at the University of Glasgow. My eye level was about two feet off the ground and going through the department's museum section with its elephant skeleton and stuffed wild cats in huge glass cabinets was a million times more exciting than the thought of a visit to Disneyland. You could smell it too, dank clouds of formaldehyde hanging above the frog-filled sinks.

I remember the two rooms that contained the electron microscope and the three that housed the faculty's new computer. Another room contained nothing but rats in cages. One day an extraordinarily obese female lab technician ladled an assortment of rats on to my folded arms – pink, black, albino, they crawled all over me. The room next door was full of cockroaches that covered the walls, floor and ceiling like glossy black paint, paint that undulated and shimmered. I remembered it with a shudder of satisfaction as I lit my Golden Virginia on the rocks of Pladda fifteen years later.

Heard Chunking from Rangoon to Mandalay

'If any of that hair gets in my food I'll cut your fucking balls off.'

Those were the very first words I heard Stretch speak. He was addressing them to me, down on the jetty as the little rowing boat pulled off with its cargo of Duncan, Ronnie, Comet the dog at the helm and Big Tam at the oars. It sat precariously low in the water and seemed to wobble, rather than glide, across the bay. My waves of farewell were curtailed by Stretch's gruff handshake and opening lines. 'And a very fine day to you too, sir,' I thought to myself, shafting him a teenage scowl I had been saving for the occasion.

Beside him, an elderly fellow with metal-framed spectacles and milk-white hair passed the bags up to Finlay who today was in charge of the tractor. 'The Professor' had been aptly nicknamed since by his appearance he could easily have been a retired Oxford don. Stretch was big in the muscular sense of the word with long dark hair and a lantern jaw. I later discovered he had converted his tiny room on the lighthouse into a small but functional gymnasium and would work out half the night when he wasn't tending the lamp. One week later we would be standing on the same jetty and he'd shake me warmly by the hand and, slapping my back, tell me it had been a real pleasure working with me – but it took a few days and nights to bring him round.

The turning point came one night when I had woken him up for his 2 a.m. Rembrandt and stayed the allotted extra half an hour. He was a man of few words. Even less that you would care to repeat. It was my second night of driving the lighthouse on my own. The day before, on the six till ten watch, I lit the lamp by myself and set the reflectors in motion. I knew the others were all downstairs watching *Mastermind*. That was a kind of safety net for me, I suppose. As I left the room clutching my box of Swan Vestas matches, The Professor had been scoring well on 'The Life and Times of Samuel Palmer and the Shoreham Ancients'.

But the next night I was left totally alone once Finlay went to his bed at 10.30 with the encouraging words that 'You'll be fine, laddie. Whatever happens, worse things happen at sea.'

It was a strange feeling being alone on the lighthouse. Not a fishing boat in sight and only a few lights still burning in the distance on Arran. I went out on the rim many times as it was a pleasant night. But I especially went out at midnight to check that all the other lights were burning, from Holy Isle to Ailsa Craig. Everything was as it should be.

And so every half an hour I wound up the weight and checked the air pressure to the paraffin. I stayed in the light room all the time, not wanting to be too far from my duties. I had a pile of books to keep me awake. I also brought up an old school jotter, a sketchbook, and my tobacco.

But when Stretch came on watch he wanted to check that everything was in order. He was gruffly satisfied that it was. I had a strong pot of tea ready for him – Finlay had told me he liked it that way – plus the usual biscuits and cheese.

'Ahm no' a great talker,' he said. 'So you can awa tae yer pit. Ah don't care.'

'I'll sit up for a bit and finish my tea,' I replied, although I was dying to crawl between the sheets and get my five hours' sleep.

A long silence followed. Eventually I noticed Stretch pull something metal from the pocket of his reefer jacket. I thought at first it was a tobacco tin, then perhaps a knife . . . But when he put it to his lips I realised it was a small mouth organ.

He started quietly at first and it was hauntingly weird, like an old Scottish lament. Both hands cradled the instrument against his face and he seemed able to get music from it that sounded like distant bag-pipes skirling in the wind.

Then he sat forward, elbows on knees, and blew harder. For a moment I wondered if he would wake the others, but the walls were thick and anyway they were used to sleeping through hours, sometimes days, of the foghorn blowing. It was an old blues number and it only took a few bars for me to recognise it. 'Million Lonesome Women', I thought to myself.

'Faan-tastic,' I murmured when he'd finished. 'Where did you learn to play like that?'

'At sea. Trawlin',' he said, and for the first time there was a glimmer of friendliness in his voice.

'I've got a copy of that back in Dundee,' I said. 'Sonny Boy Williamson on harmonica.'

'Joe Williams on vocals and guitar,' he trumped me. 'Recorded in Chicago, Illinois, 1947.' Game set and match to Stretch. But at least he was now speaking to me and not threatening to separate me from my little testosterone machines.

'Pour us another mug of tea and have one yoursel',' he said.

'There's no much of you but at least you make a reasonable mug o' tea. No' like yon Duncan. Makes it like he wis payin' for it himself. He's nae frae ony planet ah've lived on is Duncan.'

'Who else d'you like?' I asked, turning the conversation back to the blues.

'All the early guys like Big Bill Broonzy, Johnny Shines, and Brownie McGhee. An' you?'

'John Lee Hooker, I suppose,' scratching my brain. I liked the blues but I'd been sort of pulled backwards into them through what was then rather pretentiously referred to as 'Progressive' or 'Underground' music. Captain Beefheart took me back to Howlin' Wolf; J.J. Cale to Mississippi Fred McDowell. And then one of those great sampler albums came out in 1969 called *Gutbucket*, famously featuring the head of a pig on the cover. It was full of old and new sounds together: Hapshash and the Coloured Coat; Canned Heat; Groundhogs; Jo-Anne Kelly; The Bonzo Dog Band, and Big Joe Williams. It was my introduction to what the blues might become. For Stretch, they didn't need to become anything, they already were.

'So did you just teach yourself?' I asked.

'Aye, an' I listened a lot.' Stretch told me how he was born in Stonehaven but moved to Aberdeen to work on his cousin's trawler. By now he'd put away his harmonica and was carving a small piece of wood, like he was peeling a potato.

'Saw some affy bad fights at sea,' he said eventually, but didn't elaborate much except to observe. 'Easiest place in the world to get rid of a body,' and his blade flashed in the light of the beacon strobing past our window. Finlay had lit a coal fire and through choice that was our main source of light – but suddenly it felt cold. Stretch had turned the standard lamp off once I'd poured the tea.

'You get awa tae yer pit,' he told me, his voice rasping like sandpaper. 'I'm going up tae the light. The sooner they make them automatic the better. Daft fucking job. . .'

The Professor turned out to be the opposite of Stretch in many ways. But they seemed to get on better with each other than Stretch did with Finlay, and I felt there was something in the past neither wanted to rake over. I didn't ask. Meal times were not so much fun during my second week on Pladda. But when I was alone with each of the keepers it was, if anything, better.

The Prof, it turned out, had been born in Dorset, near the New Forest. He'd studied history and taught in Bath for many years. He was what is known as an Occasional Keeper. He had retired to Arran on account of the many long summer holidays he had spent there, and his historical interests drew him to the west coast of Scotland, the crossroads of Pict, Celt, Viking and early Christian, not to mention the youth hostellers and the bloody midges.

Occasional Keepers might go for months without working on a lighthouse. But out of season, when there were no students like myself to call on, they were most in demand. An unexpected illness on the light, a sudden retirement or death, would call in the Occasional Keepers. The Prof was here because Ronnie was off on his holidays. Unlike the other keepers they would rarely be sent far from where they lived. The Prof's house in fact was just down the Arran coast a little, towards Whiting Bay.

'The guy's a nutter,' Finlay told me one free afternoon when he was showing me how to roast a duck and prepare all the trimmings. 'His wife is learning to drive after all these years of cycling around Bath. Well, what's the Nutty Professor doing but teaching her the highway code by flashing lights at night between Pladda and their house? Then she flashes back the answer. Morse code, ken. I'm surprised we've no had a few yachts going down in all the confusion. He got these really high powered torches from the Army and Navy Store in Glasgow. Ken the one underneath the Highlander's Umbrella in Argyle Street?'

Unlike some of the other keepers, the Prof seemed eager to know about me, asking me what I was studying, and when I mentioned art school wondering who my favourite artists were.

Like most male art students with a literary bent I went through my Salvador Dali phase while my lecturers moaned into their clenched fists, 'Not another one!' But this lead me, as it did I'm sure for others, into the first order surrealism of Magritte and Delvaux and then into the mysticism of William Blake. Further down the track I would better appreciate Marcel Duchamp and Joseph Beuys, late Picasso and early Warhol and then the hybrid styles of Rosemarie Trockel.

'So what's your favourite painting?' The Professor asked me. 'If you could choose any one to take to a desert island.'

Quick as a flash, 'View of Toledo,' I replied. ' You know the El Greco. Only seen it in reproduction.'

'And why do you like it?'

I wasn't sure. I'd never really stopped to think about it. 'I don't know,' I said. 'It's just such a great image.'

'And what makes it great?'

I thought for a moment. 'Well, I suppose I get the feeling that I'm only seeing the landscape for a split second. Like there's been a flash of lightning and suddenly everything is illuminated. Then everything will be lost in darkness again. But he captures that very moment.'

'What do you mean exactly?'

'Well the colours, the sort of acid greens and greys. There's a sort of ghost-like feeling about it,' I groped for words. 'I like his figure paintings too, the way they really seem to be expressing something, and feeling things. But "View of Toledo" is the best.'

'Agatha and I visited Toledo once. It's a remarkable place . . . not great for cycling.' He brushed back his long white hair and then polished his gold-rimmed glasses with a blue handkerchief which he pulled from the top pocket of his corduroy jacket. Of all the lighthouse keepers I met that summer he was always the most inappropriately dressed. It was six in the morning and I was just coming on duty. All his questions were probably intended to make sure that I was fully awake, but they also made me feel welcome. He had just turned off the light, but it would be my job to make breakfast for them all and make sure they woke up in time.

'The Spanish are a great people,' he continued. 'Did you know that when the Spanish Armada was defeated they had to sail their ships right up the East Coast of England, and then Scotland, through the Orkney Islands and then back south towards home down the west coast of Scotland and then Ireland and home. A lot of ships foundered. I am always keen when I am on these lighthouse stints to meet keepers who have worked in the Orkney Islands. I've even been there a few times myself. There's about seventy islands altogether, but on one of them, Westray, is where a ship from the Spanish Armada went down. The Spanish sailors settled there and were known as The Dons. They took Orcadian names and married local girls who were themselves of Viking stock. It would make a great film, probably a better novel. When Agatha and I visited we were amazed at the dark Spanish hair and blue Norse eyes of many of the islanders. Great for cycling when the wind keeps down.'

'Is that so?' I said, sleepily. Once he'd gone to bed I went outside in the hope that the fresh morning breeze would waken me up. I had with me one of John Donne's poems from an anthology I'd found on the lighthouse bookshelf. I sat on a rock looking out to sea while the lighthouse beams faded away to nothing in the light of the rising sun. The words 'mandrake root' in the second line made me think of a Deep Purple concert I'd seen at Glasgow's Electric Garden two years before.

> Go and catch a falling star,
> Get with child a mandrake root,
> Tell me where all past years are,
> Or who cleft the Devil's foot;
> Teach me to hear mermaids singing,
> Or to keep off envy's stinging,
> And find
> What wind
> Serves to advance an honest mind . . .'

I was getting good at spotting hobbies. Stretch played the mouth organ and was into wood carving. Finlay put the finishing touches to his boat in dry dock behind the fog signal during those spare moments when he wasn't indulging his other passion – cooking. The Professor liked to read a lot and could often be seen silhouetted against the sky, sitting on a distant rock at the other end of the island. He was also addicted to crossword puzzles. Not long after he arrived he spent one afternoon sorting through all the newspapers that Big Tam had brought across. He had them neatly laid out across the big dining-room table. He was after consecutive days of *The Times* or the *Scotsman*. He would arrange them in their correct order and set himself one crossword a day. Often he'd be finished by late afternoon, completing it over tea breaks and extended lunches. But sometimes he would be stuck on a clue and he'd continue wrestling with it up in the light room.

'Grey light of the Stoke Poges landscape,' he would mutter over a Jacob's Cream Cracker piled high with freshly caught crab or lobster meat. 'Grey light of the Stoke Poges landscape? Come on Peter, help me here. Seven letters.' But of course I didn't have a clue.

The tantalising thing was he knew the answer was there in the next day's paper sitting on top of the pile. 'Grey light of the Stoke . . .' It really used to annoy Finlay who on more than one occasion grabbed the next day's *Times* and put us all out of our misery.

'Look, here it is,' Finlay would announce. 'Nineteen down, dead easy – "Glimmer". Now can we get back to watching Watergate. Mitchell's on the stand again and he's really heaping shit on Kissinger. I think the balloon's on its way up.'

Very often one week can be very like another across on the mainland. From the viewpoint of Pladda even the Isle of Arran seemed like a huge mainland continent. But on the lighthouses every week seemed to be different. My second week on Pladda saw our road down to the jetty finally begun and completed. We then repaired a second smaller jetty on the opposite side of the island which could land a small boat should any problem put the first jetty out of action. And somewhere in the middle of it Finlay launched his pride and joy, the good ship *Marilyn*. It was about twice the size of a rowing boat, with a little square cabin that had windows on three sides. It had a motor of sorts that Finlay had constructed himself from spare parts scavenged over the years from various ships chandlers and scrap merchants on Arran and in Troon.

'I knew nothing about building boats,' Finlay told me, 'when I first started this project.'

The four of us were trying to pull it up onto the road we had resurfaced earlier in the week.

'Even less now,' Stretch muttered darkly, though he was taking the main weight of the hull while we guided it on the bogey from behind. I caught something about 'a fucking chicken coop' which I'm glad Finlay missed. He was being given a lesson in the history of clinker boat building from the Professor as the two of them struggled together at the stern. Finlay had his Greek fisherman's cap pushed back on his head and his pipe clenched tightly between his teeth.

'Ah, she's a wee beauty,' he announced once we had her in position at the top of the hill.

The new road that stretched ahead of us was a bit of a disaster. There had been sand and gravel and rock chips and tar to put on in a certain order. We all knew the tar should be poured on last but we must have got some of the other ingredients in the wrong order. Either that or we tried driving back on the tractor too soon, for we'd only driven a few yards when we looked behind us and saw a tractor-wide swathe of road lifting up behind us like a giant black wave.

'Jesus!' Finlay shouted, 'Stop the fucking engine.' And Stretch jolted us to a halt. It was like watching a living cartoon and I half expected Roadrunner to emerge from behind a rock.

We managed to reverse it back into place and decided that we'd leave the tractor where it was and not do anything for at least forty-eight hours. That time was now up as we stood poised at the top of the hill with Finlay's speed-boat. We were going to attempt to get her to the bottom without the aid of the tractor which was still where we'd left it the other day.

I'd put on a few muscles over the previous week and I needed all of them over the next quarter of an hour as we lifted and rested and dragged and pulled what I too admitted looked more like a chicken coop than a boat down the hill on the bogey.

'Thanks, lads,' Finlay puffed. 'Couldna hae done it without you. The drinks would be on me if we had any.'

'I can wait,' Stretch said. 'And mine will be a double malt. A Laphroaig.'

Once I got my breath back down on the jetty I noticed a small yacht coming into the bay, and a lone basking shark cutting though the mirrored sea.

We had a break for a smoke and then set to winching *Marilyn* up into the air and down into the sea. It was the familiar barking that made me turn round and there was Comet at the front of the yacht along with Ronnie and a group of women of various ages.

'Ah thocht you were off to Benidorm by now,' Finlay shouted across to him.

'Strike by Spanish air traffic controllers,' Ronnie shouted back. 'Laker say they can get me on an Air Ghana flight tomorrow, but there's no guarantees. Everybody's over-booked into the bargain.'

'Sounds like a real buggers' muddle to me,' Finlay observed. 'Excuse the language ladies. None of you will have met young Peter here.'

And I was introduced to Finlay's wife, his wife's sister, and Duncan's wife Effie who was the oldest in the group and cloaked in a fierce tartan shawl and yellow gumboots.

'Duncan said to tell you he could not make it on account of the bowls match – it's our people against the Seventh Day Adventists in Brodick. But he wishes you well.'

The yacht belonged to a keeper on Holy Isle who had let Ronnie borrow it for the day. The women transferred from the sailing vessel to the motor boat and Finlay hopped in beside them.

He started the motor. I prayed it would stay afloat. We all waited on the jetty waving madly as it circled the bay and puttered into the open sea.

'Fuckin' chicken coop,' Stretch said. 'I'm goin' back to ma pit. Long watch tonight.'

The Professor and Ronnie and I sat on a couple of lobster creels and watched Finlay's pride and joy grow larger and smaller and larger again as he impressed the ladies with his high-speed turns and his skills at avoiding outcrops of rock.

'Amazing what you can do with some balsa wood and some Bostick,' Ronnie said. 'I'll have to send Valerie Singleton a photo of it. Maybe they'll come up and do a *Blue Peter* special on light-house keepers' hobbies. What d'you think Prof?'

'Eh?' he said, 'I'm sorry. "Carol Gold frantically embraces the Rev. Barker". Three and six.' He'd been working on *The Times* crossword puzzle which he'd been saving in his back pocket for just such a moment. 'Must be an anagram of "Carol Gold".'

Ronnie threw a stick for Comet who chased it across the beach and ran barking towards his friends the oyster catchers, as if to say 'surprised to see me back so soon?'

The Prof's eyes lit up in delight. 'That's it. "Dog Collar". Should have got that right away.' But the anxiety was soon back with twenty-one down, 'Heard Chunking from Rangoon to Mandalay.'

Great Chieftain o' the Pudding Race

'A sheep's stomach? And where am I going to get a sheep's stomach from?' I asked in a desperate voice. From inside my skull I could feel my eyeballs bulging outwards.

'Look over there, son,' Stretch commanded gruffly. And through the kitchen window, in the light of the darkening sky, I could see the field of scrub and heather that was home to Farmer Harris's recently shorn sheep.

'He always lets us slaughter one in return for clipping them. Usually Finlay would do it, but he's on leave so it's up to you to make the haggis as you are on at two this morning and you'll need the full four hours for the butchery and the cooking.'

'Ahm no' killing a sheep,' I declared, more than a wee bit hypo-critically as I'd probably eaten half a flock over the past twenty years.

'I'll take care o' that,' Stretch reassured me. 'I'll use the blood to make some of the best black pudding you've eaten this side of Union Street. Then later in the week the Professor will do his rack of lamb. If there's enough left over you'll be on biryani duty for the weekend's curry. You ken that Aberdeen's the home of the black pudding?' he asked, by the way. 'Anyway, you just help me cut her up. We'll need both the large and the small stomachs, and the eyes, the liver and the heart. And when you've got her boiling, mind to leave the wind-pipe hingin' over the pan to let oot any poisons.'

'But ah don't have a recipe,' I pleaded.

'Finlay's left his, just do it step by step,' and Stretch looked at me like the moron that I felt.

'And don't forget the oatmeal and suet, there's plenty in the cupboard.'

Suddenly it was three in the morning and the windows were as dark as coal. I was in the kitchen which looked like a collision between Noah's ark and an abattoir. There were enamel bowls full of organs I couldn't even name. The biggest pot on the lighthouse was simmering away. Every time I wiped my exhausted eyes the onion juice nipped more tears from them, and to top it all I had bits of fleece and oatmeal sticking to my fingers. 'Out, out damn fleece!' I cursed, as I rubbed my hands against the blood-spattered apron covering my precious flared jeans. I needed the arms of an octopus and the brains of an infantryman to get through this, I thought. The old timer on the cooker was ringing behind me as I thrust my hand deeper inside the elastic of the larger of the two stomachs on the bench in front of me. The sheep's eyes felt like testicles inside the mash of bran and suet. And the ringing kept on and on until I finally awoke to the realisation it had been another coming-of-age nightmare about my cooking deficiencies. The ringing was Stretch to get me up for my 2 a.m. watch, and I had no bigger worries than eating a few cuts of cheddar cheese on sweet Abernethy biscuits.

I'd been having these nightmares for a while. Strangely, as my cooking skills actually improved – as I moved confidently from omelettes to steak-and-kidney pudding to a full roast Sunday lunch – I still fretted in my darkest dreams about what I might be called to tackle next. Finlay had in fact told me about his haggis making skills a week earlier and the Professor later quoted Rabbie Burns's 'Address to a Haggis' which had cropped up in one of his crossword puzzles:

> But mark the rustic, haggis-fed
> The trembling earth resounds his tread
> Lap in his walie-nieve a blade,
> He'll mak it whissle,
> An' legs an' arms, an' heads will sned
> Like taps o' thrissle.

What it meant, other than something to do with a haggis, I haven't a clue. I'm prepared to accept it as the gourmet dish of an impoverished nation, but I've never much enjoyed it. I was a child of the Sixties, after all, and related more to the two-syllable poetry of Jimi Hendrix's 'Hey Joe'. Although Hendrix was a bit of a sore point at the moment. Before Duncan went ashore I'd made the mistake of finally turning up the 'Star Spangled Banner' to full volume in the privacy of my own room. I'd forgotten two things. One, it was the Sabbath, and two, Duncan's room was just next door where he was doubtless praying for the souls of Roman Catholics and Watergate burglars. Either that, or he was listening to the Sunday Service on Radio 4. Whatever, he burst into my room just as I was about to pull my well-thumbed copy of *Mayfair* out of my rucksack and glowered at my ITT cassette player like Moses weighing up the size of a nearby tablet and wondering on what rock he would crack it in two.

A few years earlier, as a fifteen-year-old, I'd watched the mighty

Hendrix on *The Lulu Show* playing a live version of Cream's 'Sunshine of Your Love'. It threw the TV controllers into a complete spin, but nothing like the black rage that Duncan went into, or the mortal shame I felt for the next thirty-six hours.

My generation was the first to dream cartoon dreams – technicolour cartoon dreams. From as young as I can remember, going to sleep was always a pleasure and as soon as I slipped into unconsciousness the cartoons would begin, often with big-band, caffeine-rush musical accompaniments. Elmer Fudd, Fred Flintstone, Tintin, and of course Roadrunner all zipped though my sleeping world, but often out of character, often merging with black and white Humphrey Bogarts and Lauren Bacalls or real-life street scenes from Glasgow, like Byres Road cafés on wet Saturday afternoons, and vignettes from the Whiteinch swimming pool – hot chicken soup in a plastic cup from a post-swim vending machine – too hot, over salty. My total lack of interest in Sigmund Freud probably has more than a little to do with the fact that he lived in a pre-cartoon world and I was headed for a postmodern future. So not all my lighthouse cooking dreams were nightmares. As my island idyll continued I would occasionally have the most fabulous food-filled dreams in which Finlay Watchorn did indeed become Captain Haddock and I played the role of either Tintin or young Tom the cabin boy.

I remember one dream in which the lighthouse was situated inland, somewhere like a Welsh valley, far away from any sea or any purpose. And for some strange reason the lighthouse and its surrounding buildings had become a fashionable restaurant with Finlay as Head Chef and my good self as maître d'. I welcomed in the beautiful women and tuxedoed men as the Professor valet-parked (some dream pun on Welsh valley perhaps) their Bentleys and Jaguars. And the only light they had to eat by was the revolving beam of the lighthouse up above them. The restaurant was long and narrow and could seat nearly one hundred guests at several vast tables. Finlay had prepared a huge ox which he'd stuffed with a blue dolphin, which in turn was filled with lobster, crab, and starfish. The diners, who I somehow felt had driven in a convoy from London, ate with their fingers and did so mostly in total darkness until the broad sweep of the light illuminated their bald pates, coiffured heads, and the rims of their fine wine glasses. The waiters and waitresses were naked, save for masks of peacock feather and badger felt.

Then an air-raid siren would ring. The guests would hide under the tables, the lighthouse would explode into a burning torch and the ringing of the fire engines would again awaken me to my 2 a.m. watch and a dry mouth longing for sweetened tea and cheese biscuits.

A Brief History
of Lighthouses

'Of course the Stevensons were the great lighthouse building family,' the Professor began one morning when I was handing a two o'clock Rembrandt over to him like a nocturnal baton. I'd already got the big pot of tea brewing and was slicing up a baguette and some camembert courtesy of Betty Maglone's deli in Brodick. Finlay's wife Eunice had sent it over specially that morning in the rowing boat on account of the fact it was his birthday, but he wasn't letting on how old he was. 'Have you ever seen the Bell Rock at Arbroath?' the Prof continued. 'A magnificent piece of engineering. But again just part of a much longer history.' And over the next half an hour he gave me chapter and verse on that same history. I sat there, a young Scot, transfixed by this most liberal of Englishmen who told me more about the history of my own country in thirty minutes – or so it seemed – than I'd absorbed in six years at secondary school.

'Now most people know Arbroath,' he began, 'for their famous smoked haddock, and I'd personally recommend them with a poached egg and a glass of vodka, a fine way to start the day. However, Arbroath can tender for fame on several fronts and Robert Stevenson's Bell Rock lighthouse is but one of them.

'In 1320, this is five hundred years before the lighthouse was built, thirty-one barons and eight earls met in Arbroath Abbey which had been founded by William the Lion in the twelfth century, to sign what some call the Declaration of Independence but which is proudly referred to here in Scotland as The Declaration of Arbroath. It should be as important to you Scots as the American Declaration of Independence. It was penned, in what has been described as "vigorous Latin" by the Abbot of Arbroath, Bernard of Linton, a staunch ally of Robert the Bruce.' I could tell that this guy had once been a teacher by the way he slipped into his conversational lecturing tone like a seal into the sea.

'The Declaration was a patriotic torpedo aimed at Pope John who, unlike his predecessors who recognised the independence of Scotland, backed English claims to its northern neighbour. Now our old friend Bernard of Linton did not mince his words but put them forward like a slab of blue nationalist meat. I memorised them once for a lecture at the Arran Women's Institute, let me see if I can remember,' and he sucked his pipe and looked like he might go into a trance:

'Robert I brought salvation to his people through the safeguarding of our liberties. Yet even the same Robert, should he turn aside from the task and yield Scotland or us to the English king or people, him we should cast out as the enemy of us all, and choose another king to defend our freedom; for so long as a hundred of us remain alive, we will yield in no least way to English dominion. For we fight, not for glory nor for riches nor for honour, but only and alone for freedom, which no good man surrenders but with his life . . .'

'Emotive words, Peter, and in them lies every dichotomy that has ever labelled the same group terrorists by their enemies and freedom fighters by their loved ones. Solve that riddle and Palestine and Ireland will be happier places.'

'Have you ever been out to the Bell Rock?' I asked, keen to get back to the subject of lighthouses.

'Sadly no, I have only stood by the abbey, palely loitering,' he replied cryptically.

'The abbey?' I asked.

'Yes, in a sense it was the first lighthouse in Arbroath. It has a circular window known as "The Round O". It sits high up on the east wall facing out to sea. A fire would have been lit behind it and this served as a warning beacon to ships out at sea. To all intents and purposes it was a lighthouse six hundred years before Stevenson won his first lighthouse commission.'

'But the real hazard, Peter, was really twelve miles out at sea. It is a hull-shattering rock that was known as "The Inchcape Rock", and many a life was lost there. Eventually one of the Abbots placed a warning bell on it and in time it became known as The Bell Rock. Do you know the poet Robert Southey?' he suddenly asked. And to my shame, me with my hobby of poetry, I could not think of a single thing he had written. The Professor quickly put that to rights.

'When the rock was hid by the surge's swell,' he began, tilting his head backwards and staring at a spot on the ceiling:

> 'The mariners heard the warning bell;
> And then they knew the perilous rock
> And blessed the Abbot of Aberbrothock.'

'Fine lines. And it was a fine lighthouse that Stevenson built. It is now the oldest lighthouse to have been in continuous use in the British Isles. Ask Finlay about it. He and Ronnie have both spent time on it. It was the first of eighteen lights that Robert Stevenson constructed. Can you imagine what it must have been like? We're talking way back in 1806. For most of the day the rock was totally submerged under water and these men were out there in their boats trying to construct a tower from such a base. Then there was the rest of his family, a real lighthouse dynasty of sons, grandsons and nephews – Alan, David, and Thomas. Between them they built nearly sixty lights, an amazing feat. Thomas was the youngest son, and *his* son was Robert Louis Stevenson who wrote *Treasure Island*. A remarkable family. Robert Stevenson is up there with Isambard Kingdom Brunel and Thomas Eddison. He also designed canals, bridges, railway wheels, you name it. Wait till Hollywood discovers him, what a film that will make. Probably won't happen until after the last light has been automated though, until people really realise what they have lost – the human factor as Graham Greene calls it.'

'It's strange to think that there are lighthouses all over the world, it's like a universal language,' I said, philosophically.

'It's certainly a visual language,' the Professor agreed. 'Before the Pharos of Alexandria was built, Celtic cavemen off the coast of Wales would take to the open sea in coracles of skin and reed while their women-folk built fires along the shore to guide them home. Then there was the Colossus of Rhodes. It was a giant statue with lights burning in its eyes. It straddled the harbour entrance and allowed even the tallest of ships to glide in to port beneath its towering legs. It was destroyed by an earthquake. I've heard it being described as a male version of the Statue of Liberty, legs akimbo and torch raised high.'

'I've been up the Statue of Liberty,' I said, and I could see the surprise in the Professor's face. 'I can't remember anything about it though. When I was eighteen months old my father got a sabbatical trip to Berkeley in California for a year. He's a zoologist, he discovered a new insect in the desert, called it *California Berklei*. He could have named it after himself like most entomologists do, but he never cared for the limelight. He and my mother and I sailed to New York on the Queen Elizabeth, in 1954. I'm told we went up the Statue of Liberty but I can't remember any of it.'

'Did you know it was a lighthouse?'

'The Statue of Liberty? I thought it was just a big public sculpture.'

'No, no, no. President Cleveland, back in 1886 wrote to the American Treasury that "The Statue of Liberty Enlightening the World be immediately placed under the care of the Lighthouse Establishment and be maintained as a beacon under the regulations pertaining to such beacons." And now it's time for me to go and wind the light or we'll all be out of a job,' the Professor was on his feet, and I was glad to be off to my bed where I dreamed strange dreams of Robert the Bruce sailing into New York harbour beneath the outstretched legs of the Colossus of Rhodes.

Years later I found a poem by the great Glasgow poet Edwin Morgan which had been written in 1973, the year I worked on the lights. It is a poem about the revolutionary hero who came after Bruce and Wallace but before Sean Connery and Billy Connolly – the Red Clydesider John Maclean. In 1917 Lenin made him Bolshevik consul for Scotland but he remained his own man for a' that. A son grown strong on the failure of Scotland to fully deliver to herself all that the Declaration of Arbroath promised. 'I am not prepared to let Moscow dictate to Glasgow,' it begins. And a few lines further on there is even a reference to lighthouses:

> 'Maclean wanted neither the maimed ships
> nor the paradox of not wanting them
> while he painfully trimmed the lighthouse lamp
> to let them know that Scotland was not Britain
> and writs of captains on the Thames
> would never run in grey Clyde waters.'

Three nights later the Professor and I found ourselves facing each other over a plate of cream crackers and a saucer of warm lobster meat. This time I was going on watch and he was looking forward to his bed. It was six in the morning and the sun would soon be rising, which is always a glorious sight from the rim of any lighthouse. Our conversation about lighthouses continued as if it had never been interrupted.

'Then there was Christopher Columbus's uncle. Yes, Uncle Antonio was a keeper of the great light at Genoa in Italy where he began his first watch in 1449,' the Prof slipped into his oratorical style. 'And Charlemagne's son, he too was a keeper. He was known as Louis the Pious, and here we're going back to the ninth century, can you imagine, the ninth century? He built the first lighthouse on an island called Cordouan in France. Then there was the mad Roman Emperor Caligula. He was responsible for the lighthouse at Dover. He ordered it to be built in the first century AD, and built another one on the opposite side of the channel on the French coast, but not before he had a joust with Neptune, King of the Ocean. Caligula waited by the sea, or so the story goes, and of course Neptune never turned up for the fisticuffs, so Caligula declared himself the winner. The Dark Ages took a hold of European life not long after the Fall of Rome, and do you know, Peter, they were aptly named because throughout the Dark Ages hardly a lighthouse burned.'

This lighthouse diaspora was spreading backwards through time and space in an alarming fashion. What had started as an interesting summer job was becoming a mystical vocation. I was increasingly feeling that I was becoming a member of one of the most select clubs in history. My induction into the freemasonry of lightkeeping was brought right up to the present with the Professor filling me in on current practice.

'"R plus four," is what all keepers dread,' and he spoke these words with great foreboding. '"R" stands for "relief day"' which every keeper on a rock or uninhabited island looks forward to. But look forward is not strong enough a term. Craves, like an addict craves nicotine or strong opiates. Craves the return to city lights and the warmth of the family bosom, the company of friends. "R plus four" stands for "four days without relief" when the deadline to relieve the shift is abandoned because of bad weather.'

'What happens then?' I asked, fearing I had already guessed the answer.

'That is when the lighthouse crew must face a consecutive spell of duty, and wait another month for the helicopter or the ship to take them home.'

When the Professor had gone off to bed I fished out the old, battered copy of *Treasure Island* that he'd handed me from the lighthouse bookshelf after our last talk about the Stevenson family and their lighthouse dynasty. How much had they influenced the imagination of young Robert Louis Stevenson? I went up to wind the light. Then I took the little wooden chair out on to the rim of the light, pulled my donkey jacket tight around me, and in the golden light of the rising sun began to read about the arrival of The Old Sea Dog at the Admiral Benbow:

. . . I remember him as if it were yesterday, as he came plodding to the inn door, his sea-chest following behind him in a hand-barrow; a tall, strong, heavy, nut-brown man; his tarry pigtail falling over the shoulders of his soiled blue coat; his hands ragged and scarred, with black broken nails; and the sabre cut across one cheek a dirty, livid white. I remember him looking round the cove and whistling to himself as he did so, and then breaking out in that old sea-song that he sang so often afterwards:
'Fifteen men on The Dead Man's Chest -
Yo-ho-ho, and a bottle of rum!'

I was hooked.

It took a few watches of driving the lighthouse on my own to get into the rhythm of being a fully-fledged lighthouse keeper. The good-humoured camaraderie of the day and the broken stretches of sleep combined with the solitary midnight vigils to produce a state of being quite unlike any other. Yet it was the one-on-one meetings at ten, two, and six that formed the most magical memories.

My last night on Pladda I was woken by Stretch just before two in the morning. Can you imagine what that feels like? To get out of your bed in the cold and the dark with half-formed dreams of tropical islands crashing all around you, mouth as dry as an old cement pit. To stumble into your clothes with a mouthful of tiredness and eyelids that keep re-sealing, pupils rolling backwards into unconsciousness. And then to slump into an armchair and be soothed awake by a harmonica and a mug of strong tea.

'I wonder where they'll send you next?' Stretch said to me. 'It was the training I enjoyed the most. Always on the move. I liked that.' I'd never heard him this talkative. He had swapped his mouth organ for his knife and was whittling away at the same bit of wood that he'd been working on all week. Between his knuckles, from time to time, I got flashes of a pair of breasts and a tail. The wooden curve of soft hair.

'If they give you the chance of Orkney, take it. It's fucking wonderful up there,' he advised. 'Specially this time of year. If you get a light on one of the inhabited islands they're aye round chapping on the lighthouse door inviting you to parties and ceilidhs. I remember someone was getting married once and they just put a wee sign in the post office, "All Welcome". Then the bride's father came along to the light with some French champagne and a plate of salmon. Magic people.'

'I've never been much further north than Inverness,' I said. 'I stayed at a youth hostel once called Carbisdale Castle. It was a huge place, with a disco in the basement and a billiards room.'

'Well, next time, see you keep going right up to Thurso and catch the ferry to Stromness. There's more wonderful things than castles and discotheques up there.'

'Can I ask you something Stretch?'

'Depends what it is.'

Well . . . there wasn't an easy way to put it. 'How did you get your name? Stretch. It's very unusual.'

'Glad you asked. No one else has, never understood why. You'd have thought they'd be curious, like. It was years ago. Me an' ma mates on the trawler had a syndicate and we had a wee win on the pools. No' a fortune, ken. But a few thousand each once it wis divvied up. I spent mine on women and booze mostly. The rest I frittered away. But no' before I bought an air ticket to Chicago. Always wanted to go to the home of the blues. My cousin, who wis skipper, came too and as a surprise for me he hired a stretch limousine to ferry us aboot all week. We lived like kings and somewhere in the middle of it all he started calling me Stretch, after the car like. Name stuck like, but I don't mind it.'

Throughout his tale he'd kept carving the little bit of wood. Eventually he stopped and looked it over.

'Here, this is for you. Now get off to bed, you'll be a travelling man the morn.'

And he passed over what he'd been carving all week. It was a mermaid. Later, as I turned it over in all its primitiveness in my hand, it made me remember a poem by John Arden, about a sailor coming home from the sea and looking forward to 'living by green trees on the green face of a hill'. But the outlandish wife he brought home 'both dangerous and proud', turned out to be a mermaid. 'You could tell her by her scaly tail from a hundred wives in a crowd.' Very quickly they conceived, and:

The son was like a whiting-fish with his tail curled through his eye:
She looked at him with a frozen heart and said, Lay this one by . . .

Shore Leave I:
A Surfeit of Choice

'Isn't it very lonely living on a lighthouse?' Over the years I've been asked that question many times. It's often come up at job interviews, and in the early stages of new relationships. It was never lonely on any of my lighthouses. Quite the opposite, I had some of the best company in the world. Good men with great tales to tell. I've been much lonelier, by contrast, living in a bedsit in central London, transiting in Hawaii for three days, or roaming the Canary Islands out of season with no Spanish and only the company of Paul Theroux and Graham Greene in my backpack. The hard thing was adapting to being back on the mainland. Adapting to cities, towns, villages, open countryside . . .

Even after only two weeks on Pladda – *two weeks in space, two weeks in prison, two weeks in hospital, two weeks on a desert island, two weeks in Vietnam* – fourteen days can easily stretch to a Heavenly or Hellish eternity – I had grown accustomed to a more simple life yet a more complex routine.

I've since heard of several cases of different lighthouse keepers in various countries who turned down their shore leave and annual holidays because they could not face 'the real world'. For them contentment and well-being were to be found on a friendly rock in an ever-changing ocean.

All things are relative. Suddenly I was back in Brodick waiting to catch the ferry to the mainland. What had appeared to me two weeks earlier as a tiny coastal resort now took on the dangerous dimensions of Gotham City. Cars flashed past, strangers jostled to cross the road to the bakers, the pub, the newsagent, the Crazy Golf Course, the lawyers, offices, the ice cream van. Suddenly there were so many choices. So much noise. Screaming children instead of screaming gulls, the bark of news vendors instead of seals. So many choices . . . so many decisions. You had a craving for a Mars Bar? No problem, just go into a shop and buy one. A fish supper? Get one in the wee restaurant on the waterfront. Watching a movie? *Barbarella* was back by popular demand at The Empire. Going for a long walk? Roads stretched in every direction and beyond them hills and mountains. No longer was I limited to my island acre. And as for company, well if I wanted to I could lift the phone and arrange to meet a group of friends later that evening, down in Byres Road, once I got back to Glasgow. And that's exactly what I did.

We gathered in the back room of the Rubaiyat, on the corner of University Avenue and Byres Road. Some of you will know it. Inside the mirrors were etched with the poetry of *The Rubaiyat of Omar Khayyamm*, aka 'the Voltaire of the East'. Uncle Omar was a dab hand with the mathematics and the astronomy. In his verses the first, second, and fourth lines shared the same rhyme, while the third does its own thing.

And so it was that Dave, Keith, Stuart, Arthur and myself drank our dark pints of export in the narrow back room, talking of world politics, local football, Watergate, and the latest offerings from the

Grateful Dead and Santana. Jim and Douglas had hitched down to the Reading pop festival and were expected back any day. Most of us had gone through school together, some from the age of five. All were now engaged in some kind of higher education and trapped in the eternal present. Most had made the easy journey from the Boy Scout movement with its love of the outdoors and adventure to the hippy movement with its similar concerns. The sociologists debated the political stance of the Bader Meinhof group and the IRA while two years earlier they had been more interested in the English cricket tour of Australia. The artists spoke of Kurt Schwitters, Duchamp, and the Futurists, where previously they had romanticised the Renaissance and Vasari's tales of everyday Tuscan life. If anything had politicised us – and it had – it wasn't so much the big, unpicturable events such as the bombing of Cambodia or the tanks rolling into Czechoslovakia, but the smaller more identifiable atrocities – the Mai Lai massacre, the shooting down of Kent State students by the American National Guard, the self-immolation of Jan Pallach in Wenceslas Square.

I leaned back on my chair and silently thought of Duncan and Ronnie and Finlay Watchorn on Pladda, where I had woken up that morning. Already I missed them. I thought of Stretch playing his mouth organ, and the Professor eloquently outlining the mystical inner worlds of William Blake and Samuel Palmer, then desperately wondering aloud, 'Seven letters, "Heard Chunking from Rangoon to Mandalay", it could be "Burmese", but why? No, doesn't fit . . .'

I looked through the smoke to the etched mirrors on the opposite wall of the pub:

> That Moving Finger writes;
> and having writ,
> Moves on . . .

I felt I had moved on too. I no longer felt like a student. But I didn't know if I wanted to be a lighthouse keeper for the rest of my life. We finished our drinks and the others were going on to a party. I couldn't face that many people in an enclosed space, and I was suddenly feeling very tired. I headed towards Crow Road and my parents' house and was soon fast asleep. But not for long. At 2 a.m. I leapt out of bed thinking I was late for my watch. But something was wrong . . . and then I remembered . . . and the anxiety folded into a deep and contented sleep.

This would happen on many nights, and not just after my first lighthouse. With it came the warm, luxurious feeling of knowing I could stay in bed, sleep for another six hours . . . damn it, why not ten . . . Bliss!

And then there were the dreams. Dreams that I still enjoy. Dreams of islands rising out of blue seas that reflected the golden setting sun. Dreams of gliding across those waters in a rowing boat with William Blake at the helm and Samuel Taylor Coleridge pulling up a lobster creel . . . lost scenes from *The Hunting of the Snark*.

On the morning when I left Pladda it was just such a beautiful day. Big Tam picked me up from the jetty and Stretch played a few bars on his harmonica as the boat pulled away. Finlay and the Professor shouted farewell and the big basking shark that had been circling the bay all morning followed us right across to Arran. I realised with great excitement that it was playing with us, diving far under the rowing boat and coming up on the other side, then down again to emerge opposite. And so it wove its way across the sea as I began my travels from a tiny island to a medium-sized one, and from there to the even bigger one of the mainland.

A few days later I travelled back to Dundee and the comparative squalor of my bedsit. Lachlan Fairbairn would have been proud of it, I thought. With a newly acquired lighthouse keeper's eye for detail and love of the spick and the span I set about cleaning it up. As expected, I was requested to part company with the art school. A friend had set up my work for me – paintings, sculptures, drawings, graphics, textiles, anatomy, photography, all the many subjects that make up the life of a first year art student. But the staff knew I had gone AWOL, and I remembered Ian Fearn's words, 'You'll probably get a second chance at art school, but this will be your only chance to be a lighthouse keeper.'

So there were no regrets. But there were no plans either.

On the hall table of Greenfield House I found a small stack of letters and a package containing a pair of 'SAS Approved' binoculars I had ordered from *Exchange and Mart* at least six weeks previously. They might come in handy one day.

Amongst the bills and the postcards I came across an envelope with that wonderful lighthouse watermark on it. My next posting, I thought. I wonder where I'm off to now? I tore open the envelope and discovered that no, it was something even more welcome, it was my pay cheque. Physically it was twice as big as a normal cheque. Large enough for the Gothic script 'Commissioners of the Northern Lights' to run along the top and for a lighthouse and its beam to cut across from left to right. It was made out for a handsome amount of money. I had been so busy learning and enjoying my new skills that I had forgotten that I was also being paid to do the job. I went straight to the bank and paid it into my account.

'So what are you going to do?' Lincoln asked me. We were having a curry in an Indian restaurant on Perth Road.

'Work on the lights for the rest of the summer,' I replied, my mouth full of naan bread. 'Maybe longer. I want to try and write a novel.'

'Well, you're looking good on it. I've never seen you look so healthy.'

Lincoln was about to leave himself, to work as a *ghillie* on an estate in the far north-west. He was only a year older than me in age, but seemed a decade older in worldly experience. Every few years, in different parts of the world, he still re-enters my life with his own personal brand of sunshine and good cheer (like Felix Leiter in the James Bond books) and he fills me in on all his latest adventures. We both rented bedsits in Greenfield House which is where we'd met two years before. We had the basement flats then, which were as damp as a dungeon. Orange slugs used to be seen leaving the place, heading up the stairs in search of drier ground. Eventually, Lincoln and I moved upwards too. He to an attic room with splendid views across the Tay to Fife. I migrated to one of the second floor rooms overlooking Perth Road. There was an orange street light just outside my window which gave the room a warm glow at night, which I rather liked.

Lincoln is a fine landscape painter and even in his student days would take off to remote parts of Scotland with his pastels and his oil paints. We would do all-nighters together after a few swift ones at the Tavern Bar, and talk enthusiastically with seeming first-hand knowledge of Paris at the turn of the century, although neither of us had even been to France at that point.

'I've never seen you eat so much, Pete,' Lincoln observed as I wolfed down my lamb masala between mouthfuls of lager. 'Lighthouse keeping obviously agrees with you. I remember the first curry you had you picked away at it as if it might explode.'

And it was true. In fact it was in the very same restaurant on Perth Road, conveniently opposite the dental school.

During the Sixties the exotic meal of choice in Scotland – in fact the only real alternative to mince and tatties – was the

Chinese takeaway. Then by the early Seventies Indian restaurants opened like exotic orchids and nowhere more so than in Glasgow's Gibson Street, close to the university and in the centre of the Indian and Pakistani communities which go back several generations. But other cities followed and Dundee was no exception. Like most young students my first encounter with an Indian meal was looking down the barrel of a chicken biriyani which appeared to me like something that could easily feed a family of five. Battlements of saffron-coloured rice rose up to a fortress topped with chicken and vegetables and tiled with a roof of hot brown sauce. From Inverness to St Ives, the staid British were at last changing their eating habits as the Australian poet Les Murray described in a poem called, 'Vindaloo in Merthyr Tydfil'. In the first two lines he neatly describes the epic jet journey from the southern to the northern hemisphere, 'The first night of my second voyage to Wales, Tired as rag from ascending the left cheek of Earth'. And what do they do? They take him for a curry. To the Bengal.

Lincoln and I staggered back to Greenfield House after a nightcap in the Queens Hotel where, I seem to remember, we'd unsuccessfully tried to chat up a couple of nurses from Anstruther. I longed for some female companionship.

The next day I went round to my landlady's baronial mansion and paid two weeks' rent in advance. Then I packed my rucksack. Then I phoned Suzy.

Suzy looked like the twin sister to Marc Bolan from T-Rex. Black curls of hair, platform shoes and a kaftan. She was a sociology student I'd met at a party at Stirling University where a large number of my old school friends were studying. We'd become great friends, and that was the problem. We were *only* great friends.

I guessed correctly that she'd be back in Dundee spending the summer with her family in Broughty Ferry.

'Do you fancy hitching to Amsterdam?' I asked her. To my surprise she quickly agreed.

We set off the next day, very early, from the far side of the Tay Bridge, and almost immediately a Christian-Salvesen truck stopped. We hopped in. And so began an adventure very different from the lighthouses. I was determined to make the most of my shore leave.

By nightfall we were in Harwich and had missed the last ferry to the Hook of Holland. Suzy used her immense powers of persuasion on a couple of truck drivers in the terminal car park who agreed to share the two bunks in one cab and let us use the other.

'You sure you don't want me in beside you, warm you up a bit?' I asked hopefully.

'Let's keep it just as it is,' Suzy replied. 'Sex always seems to spoil my good friendships with men.' She'd already told me she fancied her sociology tutor something rotten but he was away teaching an Open University summer school, the sod.

'But I'm a poor wee lighthouse keeper on shore leave. I could get sent away for weeks next time.'

'Well, I'll write you,' she said consolingly. 'And when you get back next time I'll introduce you to my friend Rosie. I think you two would get along fine.'

'Thanks,' I said, assuming the embryonic position of the love-starved male.

I had hitch-hiked to Amsterdam several times in the previous couple of years, each time with a different friend. In a short period this most friendly of cities seemed to change from being a sort of hippy version of the School of Athens, where young Americans avoiding the draft or recovering after a tour of duty in Vietnam would meet with their European counterparts and plan distant utopias from which all politicians, businessmen, and people over thirty would be banished, to a seedier cross between Times Square and London's Soho. At that point I stopped going there until I re-discovered its previous charms in the heady Eighties.

But the common meeting place back then was the Sleep-in. These were huge warehouses with hundreds of bunk beds stretching for what seemed like miles. You could stay there for the equivalent of about twenty-five pence per night and they sold good, cheap food. There was a large communal living area where people lay about on green foam mattresses and were entertained by liquid light shows and the constant background music of the Byrds and Bob Dylan by day, the Velvet Underground and the Doors by night.

Suzy and I explored the city on foot. We queued to get into the Rijkmuseum and trooped past Rembrandt's night watch with all the other tourists. I told Suzy about my new definition of a night watch, but she just wanted to know why there were no female lighthouse keepers. 'I don't know,' I replied. 'I'd vote for it in a flash. You know I would.' Course I would.

I remember one day it rained so hard that we took shelter under the awning of a cinema, and when we saw they were screening *The French Connection* we bought two tickets and entered the world of Popeye Doyle. It was a great movie and it was in English with Dutch subtitles, which was fine until you got to the bits which were spoken in French and normally had English subtitles. They of course now appeared in Dutch. I could just hear Finlay Watchorn describing it as 'a real buggers' muddle'.

Much of the talk at the Sleep-in was about Vietnam. There were a few Americans there with high-powered college degrees who had shot quickly through the ranks and just as quickly become totally *one hundred per cent* disillusioned with what they had seen, with the decisions they had witnessed and especially with those taking the decisions. One told us about the 'Gulf of Tonkin' incident which the US had apparently used to deliberately kick-start the whole war. Any excuse to drive the reds even further under the bed. Most read their copies of the *International Herald Tribune* gleefully, following the long awaited come-uppance of Richard Milhaus Nixon. Would Kissinger, we wondered, ever be tried as a war criminal?

We befriended a young American who could have been Joni Mitchell's younger sister. She'd been studying at Kent State and was there the day the troops opened fire on the students. She hadn't actually seen it but she'd heard the shots. Her story unfolded amongst the incense and dried apricots and the Orientalism of the Amsterdam Sleep-in. She dropped out and joined the Hari Krishna movement, much to the annoyance of her southern Baptist parents. She did a deal with them and agreed to spend a year in Europe working as a nanny in Switzerland. But within a few weeks she had gravitated towards Amsterdam and was working a bar in the Paradiso Club, living in the Sleep-in. Every day she would watch the Hari Krishnas chanting and cymbal-clashing their way down Lauriergracht to Dam Square. But she had moved on from that too. She wanted to go to London and study acting at RADA. I wonder where she is now and how her dreams turned out.

One of the great things about travel is meeting new people in strange places. Weirder still, in my experience, is meeting someone from your own city, even if they are strangers, in a new environment. So it was with Shuggie from Drumchapel. He too was staying in the same Sleep-in in Amsterdam and we met while queuing for one of the ten toilets that serviced five hundred back-packers, all of whom needed to shit at the same time. Many of us carried our own toilet rolls and knew to arrive half an hour before we expected to drop anything serious. 'What do you think of *Dark Side of the Moon*' he quizzed me about the new Pink Floyd album that had been released earlier that year. 'Crap,' I replied honestly. 'Not a patch on *Ummagumma*. That's their best album. You cannae beat "Set the Controls for the Heart of the Sun".'

'Ahm with you on that,' Shuggie agreed. 'Though the best track's "Careful with the Axe, Eugene". No two ways about it.'

'"Granchester Meadows" is pretty damn fine too,' I returned. 'But what about Al Stewart, are you intae him?' And so we went on a wee banter as the queue ahead of us gradually diminished. Al Stewart led us on to Jerry Yester and Judy Henske, and from there it was but a short jump to Dave Van Ronk and then the Fugs. 'You intae Lenny Bruce?'

'Ahm I intae Lenny Bruce?' Shuggy replied in amazement. 'Ahm his biggest fan.'

'Make me a malted,' I parried.

'You're malted,' he came back, quick as a flash of Lower East Side steel.

Lenny Bruce was not just the world's greatest and most dangerous stand-up comedian, but was also the prophet of peace who famously said 'Thou shalt not kill *means just that*.'

Only five guys ahead of us and hopefully they only wanted a piss. Inevitably, we got to Vietnam. I suspect via Country Joe and the Fish. Vietnam was both the first and the last television war. Before it, nothing was really televised at all. After it, wars became so short they only lasted a few days or weeks. Not proper wars at all. But Vietnam went on for nearly a decade, affecting a whole generation whether they lived in America, France, Germany or Scotland – Talkin' 'bout My Generation. The Baader Meinhof,

Ulster, Biafra, and Watergate came and went, but Vietnam was the backdrop that played alongside every single Beatles track from start to finish, from Hamburg to Abbey Road and beyond – well, at least as far as 'Imagine'. As a generation we stopped buying newspapers and watching television because of Vietnam. Biochemistry graduates from Cambridge with first-class honours degrees, or budding concert pianists in Sweden, grew their hair long, and dropped out because the world was going to Hell and the older generation were doing nothing about it. And you didn't have to be there to be psychologically cauterised by it, you just had to be young and anywhere on the planet – Sydney, Milan, Toronto – to know it was wrong and to see the apocalypse we were headed for. And so, ostrich-like and unable to do anything about it, we decided to enjoy ourselves and to celebrate peace rather than the Dow Jones. 'What about the Edgar Broughton Band?' I asked Shuggie.

'Saw them at the Maryland a couple of years ago, you know up from Sauchiehall Street?'

'I was there too. Right beside the art school. Great set. My hearing's never been the same since.'

And once again rock music pushed Vietnam into the background but not out of sight. Not for a long while yet.

And so it was in those strange, transient times. A few days later we hitched back to Scotland and found, when we did our arithmetic, that the whole trip, including the ferry to the Hook of Holland, had cost us sixteen pounds each. We celebrated our return with a fish tea at the Deep Sea restaurant on Perth Road.

When I got back to Greenfield House there was only one letter waiting for me on the hall table. But it was the one I had been hoping for. I tried to open the envelope without ripping the embossed lighthouse on the back flap and savoured the slow unfolding of my instructions. Would it be Orkney, or the Bell Rock, or Skerryvore?

No, it was going to be Ailsa Craig, just across the water from Pladda. That was fine by me.

AILSA CRAIG

Paddy's Milestone

Sydney, Australia: 26 June, 1998

I find I have a few hours to kill in Sydney before my flight south to Tasmania. I take a cab through this Anglo-Pacific city of four million people to The Art Gallery of New South Wales. It may have the dullest sounding name of any art gallery on the planet but it is one of the world's great art palaces. It sits on an apron of parkland high above the city's twin icons of bridge and opera house. Like the Kremlin, one enters almost on the top floor and descends downwards by a series of escalators. I begin in one of the upper galleries which is showing the work of four international contemporary artists – Gregory Crewdson, Tracey Moffatt, Pipilotti Rist, and Kara Walker – who between them represent Switzerland, Australia and the two coasts of America. It is the sort of mix of three continents, both genders and several media that contemporary art curators at the end of the century aim for. The exhibition is called *Strange Days* and as I walk around it I try to remember which Cream album the title comes from. I pick up a catalogue and am immediately corrected by the introductory lines from the 1967 hit by The Doors:

> Strange days have found us
> Strange days have tracked us down
> They're going to destroy
> Our casual joys . . .
> As we run from the day . . .

And as I left to descend to the next level and an exhibition of British painting called 'The Other Eden.' I realised that it was Cream's *Strange Brew* that my own jet-lagged memory had been recalling. Twelve hours before I had been in Bangkok. Thirty-six hours ago London, and before that Glasgow. I was so tired.

Memory is a cruel sorter. Some things sink to its depths never, ever to be retrieved – like the pin numbers for my various credit cards. Others are always there and accessible, like the first time I stuck out my thumb as a fifteen-year-old to hitch a lift in a car and, amazingly, it stopped. Or when I came home from the cubs one evening and I was halfway across our red-carpeted hall when my sister told me that President Kennedy had been shot. The whole scene is frozen like a snapshot – my bicycle leaning against the right-hand wall, the dark hall cabinet with its mementos, postcards and photographs, the good glass-topped table tucked underneath it to be produced on special occasions, the light above from the wrought metal shade, the smell of pancakes being cooked in the kitchen . . . all are linked forever with the death of a president. But somewhere in-between these two extremes of the forgotten and the never-to-be-forgotten are the memories that require a trigger, and once it is pulled the flood-gates open. A certain kind of cake seemed to do it for Proust, something called a *madeleine* I believe.

Egg, bacon and fried scone with a large dollop of tomato sauce do it for me, hurtling me back in my mental Tardis to early childhood Sunday mornings, before church and after games in the back lane of our terraced house in Glasgow. Other clues are visual, and as I walked around 'The Other Eden' in Sydney, past an impressive 'Zebra' by George Stubbs, past the romantic visions of Turner and the gimlet-eyed Allan Ramsay I came at last, and quite unexpectedly, to a tiny oil painting of a stretch of sea with a pudding-shaped island on the horizon. I had to do a sort of double-take, as I'd almost walked past it. I *knew* where that was. The label confirmed it: 'Ailsa Craig', painted by William Bell Scott in 1860. Like all the other works in the exhibition it was part of the Paul Mellon Collection at Yale. But that was of no immediate interest. The thing that pulled my nose right up to the canvas was a single, tiny, white, vertical brushstroke – the lighthouse on Ailsa Craig. It had been my home for nearly eight weeks. There in the air-conditioned splendour of an Australian art gallery the flood-gates opened with a vengeance and I was pulled back a quarter of a century to 1973 . . .

You have probably seen Ailsa Craig, but may not at first recall it. When The Open golf championship comes from Troon, south of Glasgow, Ailsa Craig is the island the camera frequently pans to, sitting on the horizon looking closer and smaller than its one-thousand-feet height and ten miles distance suggests. It is about the same height, but not quite as wide, as Uluru – Ayers Rock – in the centre of Australia, and rises out of an ocean of water rather than sand.

'The Craig' was for eight weeks one of my lights, with the rotating company of at least six other keepers. They would come and go on their holidays and with their illnesses while I stayed there in their stead. I think it was a record for any lighthouse keeper on Ailsa Craig – four weeks usually being the maximum. That year the golf *did* come from Troon and we sat inside the living quarters of our lighthouse and saw ourselves as others see us, from the outside, a blip on the horizon. I waved once, over the dry-stone dyke, but no one waved back. Not waving, not drowning, too busy putting, I thought. Daytime was a time for amusing thoughts and reflections like these, when life was shared with a camaraderie that might have come out of the most golden passages of *The Wind in the Willows*, or the opening chapter of *The Hobbit*.

But when it grew dark, and then darker – when mine was the only conscious human mind for miles – that is when I would climb the stone stairs to the light room with an armful of books, a pen, and my yellow notebooks. There I would read Paul Celan, Gunter Grass, and Gregory Corso, strolling round the balcony between poems, leaning on the rail, slowly, carefully, rolling a Golden Virginia, then returning to my wooden seat, warm in my donkey jacket, absorbed, entangled, in another human's mind. At three in the morning on an isolated lighthouse it was over-easy to identify with Stevie Smith, never quite sure whether my life was one big wave or a certain kind of drowning.

And then it would be morning again, and I would rein in my thoughts from across the expanding galaxy of night. The sun would rise above the cries of the oyster catchers and a shared life would recommence amongst the Kellogg's Cornflakes and the Robinson's Marmalade.

It was a full-sized fishing boat that took me out from Girvan to Ailsa Craig. The sea was choppy and I soon realised this was no little hop across the bay to Pladda. The island we were heading for just seemed to get bigger and bigger and bigger. I was being dropped off with the food, the mail, and the week's provisions.

Then the crew of six were heading off to do their day's work which would stretch long into the night and into the next day.

No longer a virgin light keeper, I knew the routine I was going into. I knew what my duties would be. And I answered with confidence the questions of the youngest member of the crew, a boy of fifteen, about the keeping of the light. I was an old hand.

From this point onwards the main revelations I would have would come from my fellow keepers and their midnight tales. Or so I mistakenly thought. There were still a few unexpected adventures up ahead.

Rock of Ages

Right from the start it was taken for granted that my training was complete. As far as my new family of fellow keepers was concerned I might already have worked on several lights. They were both down at the jetty to meet me and a third, the keeper I was replacing, was about to take his leave. More importantly, they were there to pick up three cardboard boxes of provisions and a handful of mail. In return they gave the skipper of the fishing boat a plastic dustbin full of conger eels. Brown as stout and wriggling like giant worms, they had been caught in the keepers' lobster creels and would quickly be sold on to a Chinese restaurant in Girvan.

Ross McGillivray and Euan Linklater introduced themselves, and the three of us walked back to the lighthouse. They were both in their mid-to-late thirties, both open and friendly as I found most keepers to be, but quite different in appearance. Ross, who came from Ayr, just across the water, was tall, thin and had a mop of red hair. Euan, an Orcadian, was short and plump and as I would see always seemed to have a smile on his face. Something terrible must have happened to him in the past.

We got to know each other over lunch and quickly discovered each other's hobbies. Ross was another golfer, a favourite lighthouse hobby, and I noticed a bag of clubs in the corner of the living room. When the weather was too bad to practice his swings he would retire inside and work on his family tree which he had traced back several centuries.

Euan, as a child, wanted to be an architect. His father, he told me over our ham salad lunch, died while he was in his teens and he had to go straight to work in a shipping office in Kirkwall. He never did get to study architecture. But that didn't stop him drawing up plans for buildings.

'I started with bungalows and extensions to existing buildings,' he explained in the most beautiful, soft, Orcadian accent. 'Even wee things like bus shelters – they were fun. Then I designed a lighthouse, never thinking I'd end up living in one. That led on to tower blocks, which were a novelty at the time in the big cities like Glasgow, but were never seen at all up in Orkney thank goodness. From there I went on to design concert halls and museums. None of them were ever built of course, nor are they likely to be,' he said with quiet precision, modestly curling the edge of the tablecloth with his fingers and staring askance as if looking for a pulled thread. 'Now . . . well I'll show you one day. I have my drawing table set up in my room here. It's a bit like a combination of science fiction and architecture. But it's just a hobby. Once I realised all my work would only ever exist as plans, well it really freed me up. I realised I could design *anything*. Underwater housing, floating rock stadiums . . .' It's getting nicely weird again, I thought to myself.

They in turn asked me about art school and if I had any other hobbies. 'I do a bit of writing,' I answered obliquely. 'And reading, of course. Biographies, art history, sometimes a bit of poetry.' I was coming close to being honest about my passions. But not quite there yet.

'Burns,' Ross McGillivray muttered into his ice cream and peaches. 'If you grow up in Ayr you get Rabbie Burns rammed down your throat morning, noon and night. The ploughman poet. School visits to his cottage. Usually twice a year. All our dish towels at home were covered in Burns poetry. Had to learn it by heart at school. Nae folk speak like that onymair. Mind you, my friends, they've cleaned up all his lyrics. The first verse of 'Comin' Thro' the Rye' is a scorcher and he burst into song:

> 'O gin a body meet a body,
> Comin' thro the rye;
> Gin a body fuck a body,
> Need a body cry.

'And it gets a lot hotter after that. He wrote the whole thing on a pane of glass in the Globe Tavern in Dumfries, you know. Used the diamond in his ring to etch it into the windae.'

That was my first encounter with Ross's love of historical detail which normally found its outlet in his labyrinthine family tree. I later learned this sprawled over three continents and several centuries.

I was eager to explore my new island. Euan told me that it was possible to walk right round it and, if I was fit enough, to climb to the top. Ross added that my watch that night was going to be from ten until two so my afternoon would be free. I set off straight after we'd got the table cleared and the dishes dried and stacked away.

I didn't know then that I would be on this island for the next eight weeks and by then would know it as intimately as my own childhood. I set off to walk around it.

As I'd approached it from the sea it had looked like a giant rock looming towards the sky and coming straight out of the water. You really have to be on it to realise that there is a very wide and rocky beach that runs all the way around it. Some of these individual rocks were the size of a family saloon car so in a sense one climbed around the beach rather than strolled across it. If Pladda was the equivalent of a rowing boat then Ailsa Craig was a Cunard Ocean Liner. But a liner with no passengers and only three crew. The walk around the base of the rock was over two miles in circumference. And we had her all to ourselves.

The lighthouse and its many out-houses had been built close to the sea on a very wide grassy apron. Around it ran a perimeter wall painted as white as the light itself.

There were a few derelict houses opposite the pier and in the distance I could see the foundations and rubble of many more. Later I would hear blood-curdling tales about the Irish quarrymen who lived and laboured here and produced the finest granite in the world. Much of it was destined for curling stones. They had long since gone, well over twenty years ago, and before they left they blew up their houses with the dynamite they had left over. One stayed behind and became a hermit, known to the keepers as Ben Gunn, and many a Rembrandt over the coming weeks was filled with tales about his strange life and his bizarre death.

Beyond these houses I took a path to the right and gradually noticed an incredible number of dead, half-eaten rabbits to either side of me. This continued wherever there was a grassy area. I later discovered that through a cunning ecological chain Ailsa Craig was infested with rats and the reason for that was because of the huge rabbit population. The rats ate the rabbits, and the rabbits were so abundant because myxomatosis had never been introduced to the island. On the return from my walk Euan would tell me always to keep every door firmly closed. That night, on my first watch, I understood why. My jaw dropped in amazement when I saw the rats, thousands and thousands of them, racing about in the beam of the light.

I quickly reached the base of this most unique sea mountain and began to edge around it. The wind had blown away the few remaining clouds and the dark blue of the sea met the light blue of the sky as I tracked the horizon all around the island.

Ailsa Craig is full of surprises and the next one I got was on discovering a little railway track running around the edge of the cliff. It was bigger than a toy railway track but still a miniature version of a real one. I could stand between the rails but there was not a lot of extra room on either side of my feet. Once again, I felt I was an extra in a Rupert Bear cartoon and half expected a little engine to puff around the corner with Algie the dog at the controls.

I imagined the track had something to do with the quarry and was later told it had been used for transporting the granite down to the jetty.

It took me a good fifty minutes to clamber around to the far side of the island, the opposite side to the lighthouse. I passed caves full of puffins and saw sheer chords of rock rise up to the sky. Nearer the top they appeared snow-covered but what I was seeing was not snow but the white sheen of one of the world's biggest gannet colonies. High above me over ten thousand birds were perched on the one-thousand-foot cliffs.

I was just wearing jeans, a T-shirt and some trainers. I climbed to the top of a smooth rock which was about the size of a small domestic house. I stretched out and pulled a slim volume of verse from my back pocket. I rolled a cigarette and lit it. Below me in the sea two giant rocks tumbled against each other. It was the most primeval thing I have ever heard. A sound that might have been poised to happen for thousands of years. And Duncan's words came back to haunt me: 'There's never any rush on a light-house'.

Sixty million years ago this island was a volcano, unplugged and breathing fire.

Amazingly, granite from Ailsa Craig has been found as far south as Wales – it is so unique it could not have come from anywhere else. During the last ice age a glacier twisted across Ailsa Craig, pulling samples of granite in its wake, delivering it to distant valleys hundreds of miles to the south.

The Lost World

Every afternoon, during my first week on Ailsa Craig, I explored a different part of the island. On the second day I discovered a ruined castle tower about a third of the way up the rock. I had followed an overgrown path up the steep hillside. It grew more cliff-like the higher I went.

Having dipped back into civilisation over the previous two weeks – the cars, the exhaust fumes, the forming and breaking crowds in the cities and the shopping malls, the tourists in Dam Square, the clatter of knives and forks in the Deep Sea Restaurant on Perth Road – I was glad to return to island solitude. I climbed halfway up the ruined tower and could see the tiny lighthouse three hundred feet below me. The following day I decided to go right to the top of the island, another seven hundred feet above the tower.

It was a breathless rather than a difficult climb, and a path of sorts went all the way to the top. Over the next two months I would make this climb several times and each time it would be different. On the first occasion low cloud and mist set in about six hundred feet and my bare arms suddenly felt cold and damp.

I pushed on until I reached the summit, so swathed in cloud I could only see a few yards in any direction. Eerily it reminded my of Sir Arthur Conan Doyle's *The Lost World*. Large seabirds arced out of the gloom like pterodactyls screaming as they wheeled through the soup-like atmosphere.

On other days there was no moisture and the views from the top were, in estate agents' parlance, to die for. To the south you could just make out the Isle of Man; to the south-west, Ireland; due west was the Mull of Kintyre; directly to the north lay Arran – and I searched in vain for a sighting of Pladda; to the east the hills of Renfrewshire.

I never tired of exploring Ailsa Craig. She always produced some new aspect of herself just as you thought you knew her inside out. I gradually got to know her from the sea as well, at different times going out in the little rowing boat with various keepers to pull up the lobster creels, to fish for mackerel, or just to row lazily in a three-mile circle around her.

Most days, if the weather was fine – which it usually was – I would clamber round to the beach of giant rocks on the opposite side of the island to the lighthouse. Here I would swim naked in the sea, leaving my clothes in a pile on the rocky shore. Afterwards, I would stretch out on a slab of granite and dry in the sun. There was never another soul in sight until one day when I emerged from the sea and I couldn't find my clothes. I had swum longer and further than usual and had drifted away from my starting point. Naked and dripping wet, my long hair covering half of my chest but little else, I leapt from rock to rock in search of my jeans and T-shirt; my thin arms and long wet hair flapping in the summer breeze. At the very same instant a Girvan pleasure boat rounded the north side of the island laden with twenty-odd birdwatchers who had apparently hired her for the day. Their binoculars and telephoto lenses were trained on the shore. I often wonder if I made a guest appearance in someone's photo album along with the guillemots, shags, and gannets of Ailsa Craig. The lesser-spotted lighthouse keeper, naked, attempting to fly.

Having now served on two lighthouses I was better able to build a picture of how all lighthouses might differ from each other. The 'routine' as my old friends on Pladda had described it, stayed pretty much the same. Variations were slight but significant. On some lighthouses mail was delivered every week, and this was the case on Ailsa Craig. On others it might be once a month, or with every relief.

Similarly with food. On Ailsa Craig we had fresh food delivered every Friday with the mail. Prior to this we would sit down and plan out the next week's meals. Each lighthouse keeper was allocated what to me seemed a small fortune for their 'purvey'.

Each week was a blank slate and we would do the culinary equivalent of plea bargaining with each other to make sure that everyone's taste buds were satisfied. We had legs of ham and roast beef and wonderful salads seasoned with expensive oils and vinegars. We had watermelon and pineapple, and breads studded with poppy seeds. Ice cream came in exotic flavours and was squirreled away in the deep freeze. Meat was diced and turned into hot Indian curry or steak and kidney pie. The only thing we never needed to order was fish.

We pulled that straight from the sea. It was a great summer for catching lobster, and all we pined for was a glass of chilled white wine or even a half-pint of heavy. And as the days turned to weeks over that remarkable summer, gradually, very slowly, and with many disasters along the way – such as when my glasses steamed up and I tipped a whole pot of cabbage down the sink – I learned how to cook. Not brilliantly, not with the flair of

Finlay Watchorn, but well enough for second helpings to be frequently requested.

Ross and Euan were amiable companions. Their eccentricities emerged more slowly than had my colleagues' on Pladda. I remember one day when our long, hot summer was interrupted by the most incredible downpour of rain. It lasted for hours.

That afternoon we all huddled together in the warmth of the living quarters with a big coal fire burning and a huge pot of tea on the hob.

The Open was coming from across the water in Troon and we had all been watching it over lunch at the insistence of Ross.

'It's gonna be rained off,' he predicted correctly. It was not a difficult prophecy since the rain was already lashing our windows and the wind was blowing due west, towards Troon. 'Let's watch it while we can,' he concluded not unreasonably as Euan served up haddock and chips. Half of the meal had been caught the day before, while the other half had been grown in our vegetable garden. Only the tomato and lemon had been imported.

Ross was a big fan of Norman Mair, the *Scotsman's* golf correspondent. Whenever the fishing boat came out, which was sometimes two or three times a week, he would skim through to the back section to find Mair's words of wisdom. Since Billie-Jean King predictably won Wimbledon the previous week, the sports pages of every newspaper had been filling up with golf.

And even though the newspaper coverage, by the time we got to see it, was a few days behind the live television coverage, Ross would still insist on reading out Norman's pronouncements over breakfast.

'Listen to this, chaps,' he'd say in fine imitation of a middle-class Scottish accent, although I had not the slightest idea of

Mair's nationality let alone his social standing. 'He must have writ this a few days ago. Onyway, it sets the scene: "As the Open nears, there are some strange sights and goings-on in Troon. Peter Thomson is liable to pass you with a convulsive shuddering of the shoulder that looks like a form of St Vitus Dance or maybe just the twitch . . ."'

'Lovely turn of phrase,' Euan broke in.

'Aye, you can keep your Rabbie Burns, Peter,' Ross continued, looking across at me. 'He couldnae hold a candle to our man Mair. So where was I? . . ."or maybe just the twitch but is, in fact, merely the very successful loosening exercises recommended for his strained left shoulder by Tom McClurg Anderson, a retired physiotherapist living in St Andrews. Similarly, Derek Pillage could have been excused if he edged nervously nearer the door when the champion, Lee Trevino, with the look of a man who sees visions, suddenly seized the manager's clubs and started feverishly sawing bits off them."'

We both looked puzzled as Ross continued.

'"Here again there was a rational explanation, it having come to Travino that in order to hit his irons in low, he needed a softer shaft, and the costly set Pillage had purchased in Australia three months ago was exactly what he wanted – save that they were half-an-inch too long.

"Go and buy yourself a new set," he told the incredulous Pillage. "It doesn't matter what they cost just send me the bill . . ." In addition to his woods and putter, Trevino has, of course, retained his two wedges . . ."'

Once the championship got underway, the talk was less of Trevino and Rodriguez and more of Weiskopf, Nicklaus and Yancey. They were the leaders when the thunderclouds rolled in, the punters raised their candy-coloured umbrellas, and the television commentators started to reminisce about past triumphs and failures. Ross continued reading from the *Scotsman*.

"'Pillage was not the only man Trevino surprised yesterday. For after stating that Chi Chi Rodriguez was an absolute master in a wind – a view with which Chi Chi could not bring himself to disagree – he cited the Puerto Rican as maybe the best small-ball player in all America. This, felt Rodriguez, was more doubtful since actually, "I've never played it – or hardly ever . . ."'"

'Shut up, man, and look at the screen,' Euan commanded Ross.

When they had exhausted their store of anecdotes and the BBC cameraman had tired of filming first the waterlogged eighteenth green and then the waterlogged car park, the camera had suddenly panned around 180 degrees and pointed out to sea. There on the horizon was Ailsa Craig, eventually followed by the jaunty voice-over of Peter Alliss.

'I wonder if the keepers on Paddy's Milestone are tuning in today?' and we all gave a spontaneous cheer, then self-corrected our enthusiasm with asides of 'English bampot', and 'Dinnae come oot here in yer fancy yacht'. But if truth be known we were all tickled pink, especially when he said what a great job we all did and wouldn't it be a black day when all lighthouses are automated.

'No such a bad guy, yon Peter Alliss,' Ross opined.

'A gentleman,' Euan concurred. 'An honorary Scot so he is.'

The same clouds that were breaking over Troon had been shrouding Ailsa Craig half an hour earlier, and reinforcements were queuing up to take their place. We washed and dried the dishes and hunkered down for an afternoon indoors.

I got out my watercolour paper and half a dozen bottles of ink which I'd brought with me. Euan set up his portable drawing board on the dining-room table, and Ross taped his ever-expanding family tree to the dining-room wall. He'd told me this amazing story before about how he'd traced his family back to the American Cree Indians. Apparently, or so he said, the leading negotiator between the Cree tribe and the US government in the years after the American Revolution was an Indian chief called Alexander McGillivray. *His* father was a Scottish trader called Lachlan McGillivray and his mother was half Cree and half French. 'So that makes me one sixteenth Red Indian,' Ross McGillivray exclaimed with a touching lack of political correctness. 'When I was working on Muckle Flugga with Finlay Watchorn he wouldn't let me forget it. Kept calling me Tonto and making all these Keemo-Sabi jokes,' – pronounced slowly *Keeeee Mooooo Saaaaa Baayyyy.* 'Then he said that maybe Lachlan was a family name too and maybe I was related to Lachlan Fairbairn. Wouldn't that be a scunner?'

'Jings, crivens, help ma boab.' Ross had responded in a deadpan accent.

I asked Euan how he'd got involved in his family tree and he told me it was through reading an article in the Northern Lighthouse Journal that had been reprinted from Canada's lighthouse magazine. It was written by an old keeper on a light off Nova Scotia, and had caught Euan's interest. Apparently there had always been a rumour in his family about Indian blood and he was intrigued to find out more. He got in touch with the keeper, who by then was retired and living in Florida. They still corresponded occasionally.

Back in the present, July 1973, the rain continued to pour and the television showed highlights of yesterday's golf. When they had exhausted that, and as the rain was still teeming down, the smooth tones of the BBC announcer heralded an unscheduled trip to Washington and the on-going hearing of the Senate Watergate Committee.

'Och, back to Disneyland, ' Ross commented. 'Wouldnae happen in the Soviet Union.'

'Couldnae happen in the Soviet Union,' Euan parried, and I sensed they'd visited this ground before. 'You've got to be a pretty confident democracy to go through something like Watergate.'

'But Watergate's only the bright white shiny bit at the top o' the iceberg,' Ross argued. 'It's whit's underneath that's the real crime. America's foreign policy for a start. Wee Henry and his generals. They're the ones who should be on trial.'

The broadcast which had come on to replace the golf was now itself interrupted with a newsflash and the sudden appearance on the screen of the anchorman in Washington and then the flustered appearance of White House spokesman Ronald Ziegler.

'The President is in excellent spirits,' he began.

'Sounds bad,' Ross was in quickly with his prognosis. 'Maybe the guy's thrown a wobbly.'

'The President left the White House tonight to enter Bethesda Naval Hospital,' Ziegler continued. 'Though weak and running a temperature of 102 degrees he is in excellent spirits.'

Then they wheeled on his physician, a Dr Walter Tkach.

'Whit sort of a name's that?' Ross wondered.

'I have seen his X-rays and I am confident the pain in the right side of the President's chest is viral pneumonia.'

'Bet it's a hearty,' Ross continued his diagnosis.

'I foresee no complications,' Ziegler corrected him, and it was back to the anchorman in the studio who was ad-libbing and perspiring equally profusely.

'Mr Nixon has just returned from a three week rest at San Clemente. Before entering hospital he spent the working day at the White House in discussions by phone with Senator Sam Ervin, chairman of the Senate Investigating Committee. Later he met the German Foreign Minister, Herr Walter Scheel. But it is the growing Watergate scandal that is occupying most of the President's time. He has apparently been warned that he could provoke a constitutional crisis if he continues to refuse to hand over White House papers on the bugging scandal . . .'

'Aye, the shredders will be running through the night,' Ross said philosophically.

I have fond memories of that afternoon when we all stayed indoors on account of the rain. That night I wrote it up in my little yellow notebook. I was increasingly spending my watches writing as much as reading. I had begun my novel, a work very much of its time called *Even the Rocks Have Souls*. I still have it somewhere in a cardboard box under the house, although I couldn't bear to look at it now. But it taught me many things. It taught me the discipline of writing two thousand words every night – that was the target I set myself for each watch. And later, living in a bed-sit in Glasgow on the proceeds of my lighthouse keeping, it taught me how to type. Slowly at first, like a blind hen pecking in the wrong part of the farmyard, then a little quicker but not yet with accuracy. Finally, the outer digits joined in the dance and my typing skills overtook my hand-writing abilities. Now, computer literate, I have handwriting that is as indecipherable as a Viking rune.

Up in the light chamber my novel grew in green foolscap-sized exercise books while the little yellow notebooks remained for inspirational jottings, culinary *aide-memoires*, and the day-to-day activities on the island. When I had completed my personal writing duties and my official lighthouse ones I would go out on to the rim – the lip of the light chamber – with a freshly rolled cigarette. From this vantage point I'd contemplate the sea. The rats were always there, running in endless circles in the beam of the light, like hamsters round a giant wheel. After a while I hardly noticed them.

The best nights were when various fishing fleets pulled into the side of the island to sort their catch and have a few beers. I'll never forget the first time I saw it. It was like seeing a fairground bobbing about at sea. The outline of the boats was drawn in lights, mostly white but some blue and red. The voices of the fishermen carried across clearly and amiably as cans of lager were thrown from one boat to the next.

Sometimes I'd just lean and think . . . and sometimes I'd just lean. Most watches, especially on fine nights, would see me out reading a poem at least once, out loud. My notebook-diaries tell me that Austin Clarke's 'The Straying Student' hit the right chord on the night the golf had been rained off. By three in the morning it was clear and still. As I read of '. . . a holy day when sails were blowing southward,' I knew the golfers and their commentators would awaken to a fine summer's morning.

The Island Visitors

Sometimes the world came to visit us in our isolation. Usually in the form of day-trippers from Girvan who would fill the pockets of the local fishermen for an afternoon's adventure and a trip round the lighthouse.

The boats would moor at the jetty and an assortment of ages and nationalities would troop up the path and knock on our front door.

'I cannae believe some of them,' Ross said one day when we'd had two batches through.

'Yon wee lassie with the tartan scarf, I think she was Italian, asked if there were any cafés on the island. I told her to follow the quarrymen's railway track as far as the first row of houses and she'd find a nice wee caff next door to Woolworths.'

We probably averaged about one set of visitors each week. The management at 84 allowed us, in fact encouraged us, to show them the light and give a short talk about its workings. However, accepting money for this, even as a tip, was strictly forbidden.

I remember on Pladda, Finlay Watchorn told me the story about some keepers on one of the Isle of Man lighthouses which, for obscure historical reasons comes under the aegis of the Commissioners of the Northern Lights. Apparently they were doing a roaring trade charging a pound a head and collecting money in the sort of big leather pouches that used to be favoured by milkmen, the kind that hang on a strap from the shoulder. It was not until they were all sacked that the internal investigators also discovered they had been selling on reserve supplies of mercury from the light chamber to a dodgy chemist in Blackpool.

The strange thing was, when visitors did turn up, I found myself avoiding them. You would think the desire for extra human company would have had me down there on the jetty cheering them ashore. But if they arrived when I was not on watch and when I was not required to give them the tour, I stole away – often to the ruined castle tower, sometimes to the most distant and hardest to reach beach, occasionally, if it was a hot day, to a favourite cave where I would sit reading at its entrance.

When I eventually mentioned this to other keepers they were not surprised. 'We all do the same,' they would say. 'We get used to our peace and quiet. We see enough people when we go ashore.'

But not all visitors were holiday makers slotting in a trip to Ailsa Craig between a visit to Culzean Castle or Burns Cottage.

I remember once a yacht crewed by two Englishmen pulled into the jetty. They had sailed from Cornwall to Ireland and were now breaking their journey en route to Helensburgh. They asked us on board and poured us each a large whisky. It was a good single malt too – Highland Park from Orkney. They would travel as far north as the Orkney Islands they told us, then return to Cornwall down the east coast. The drink, my first in three weeks, made my head dance like a church hall full of young farmers in Spring.

But the strangest thing was, I'd been having one of my cravings all day. Sometimes it happens that out of the blue you desire a certain type of food, and because you know there is only what's in the freezer or the pantry the craving gets worse.

It was grapes that day, I remember it distinctly. All day I had been longing for a bunch of sweet, seedless grapes. And guess what we were offered along with the whisky? Israeli grapes via a Belfast fruit shop. I'd have to try this more often, willing things to happen, and that night went to bed fantasising about Rose and Liquorice, the two female members of The Incredible String Band.

Throughout my eight weeks on Ailsa Craig various specialists visited us too. It is strange what will pull different professions to a remote island. Though not so strange once you got to know the island.

One week a professor from Aberdeen and his two female assistants arrived. I was told they were regular visitors. They came for the gannets and told us that over 5% of the world's total gannet population lived on Ailsa Craig. I was impressed.

They lived in the least dilapidated of the old quarrymen's cottages. But most of the time they spent up above the sheer cliffs, lowering each other down on ropes to ring selected groupings of birds and check the tags on others – find out where they'd come from. The bearded ornithologist told me that one of the lighthouse keepers on the Bass Rock, with whom I would later work and who confirmed the story, had once sighted an albatross. I think he said it was the furthest north such a pious bird of good omen had ever been clocked.

In those days I was a little like the character Wilson in Graham Greene's *The Heart of the Matter*, who we meet in the first chapter, in a West African colony sitting on the balcony of the Bedford Hotel with his bald pink knees thrust against the ironwork, staring out to sea. He is waiting for his gin-and-bitters and 'watching the young negresses' in the High School across the road:

> 'A black boy brought Wilson's gin and he sipped it very slowly because he had nothing else to do except to return to his hot and squalid room and read a novel – or a poem. Wilson liked poetry, but he absorbed it secretly, like a drug. *The Golden Treasury* accompanied him wherever he went, but it was taken at night in small doses – a finger of Longfellow, Macaulay, Mangan: "Go on to tell how, with genius wasted, Betrayed in friendship, befooled in love . . ." His taste was romantic. For public exhibition he had his Wallace. He wanted passionately to be indistinguishable on the surface from other men: he wore his moustache like a club tie – it was his highest common factor, but his eyes betrayed him – brown dog's eyes, pointing mournfully towards Bond Street.'

As I became more experienced as a lighthouse keeper and less self-conscious as the youngest member of the many teams of keepers with whom I worked, I began to talk about my love of poetry and to my surprise kept finding receptive audiences.

'Read us a poem,' different keepers would sometimes suggest when I had exhausted my tales of student life in Dundee and the Tavern Bar.

My own small library of books was supplemented through one of the most welcome of services that exist for the seaman and the light keeper. It was called The Seaman's Library. Every three months or so a huge chest would arrive full of books of all kinds. These would usually be chosen by an anonymous librarian in Girvan or Oban or Arbroath and sent out with the major supply vessel to all the coastal stations.

I was told it was even possible to request certain genres of books, not specific titles but types such as 'Crime', very popular, 'Westerns', even more popular, or non-fiction relating to particular hobbies – Gardening, Golf, or Harley Davidsons – many keepers were great motorbike enthusiasts and I met one who planned on his retirement to ride the length of Route 66 with his wife Peg on the back.

I burrowed and fossicked inside the big trunk and found everything from well-thumbed copies of the *Doctor in the House* series to a barely opened edition of *Das Kapital*. How had the latter got there, I wondered? Had it just been plucked at random by an over-worked librarian rushing towards a lunch in the park?

This library in a box was actually restocked while I was on Ailsa Craig. It happened when Ross and Euan left and fresh supplies arrived with the replacement keepers. I thus had two opportunities to rummage through these boxes of strange delights. They were low on poetry books but I did find a thick volume of narrative verse, and there of course was *The Rime of the Ancient Mariner*.

You know it well I'm sure, so unlike the mariner with the wedding guest I will not detain you long. But I can't resist the one mention in the epic poem of a lighthouse. It sets the scene well for what is to unfold. I once read the whole poem to Euan Linklater at two in the morning, and to my delight the weather obliged with the necessary sound effects. It was one of those great 'moments'.

> The Ship was cheer'd, the harbour clear'd—
> Merrily did we drop
> Below the Kirk, below the Hill,
> Below the Light-house top.

One day, not long after the golf had finished at Troon, a rowing boat with two photography students from Guildford in Surrey landed on our island. Had they not come, my life would have wound through other gardens and I would have chosen between different forking paths.

I can't remember their names. His project was to photograph the bird colony on the island. Hers focussed on us, the light-house keepers. She photographed us cooking our meals and making our beds, while he went off in search of gannets and shanks.

He climbed the steepest cliffs, she tracked us through our domestic and working days and nights. She was there when we lit the giant paraffin lamp and set the mirrors in motion on their huge bed of mercury. She caught us on our solitary walks around the island, dreaming our individual dreams. She caught us shaving in the cracked bathroom mirror. She captured our absorption in hobbies. A quarter of a century later this kind of photographic voyeurism would be called *Big Brother* or *Survivor*.

But the strangest thing, of course, was not that she was a photographer, but that she was a woman. She was all our dreams made flesh. At night, she and her partner camped inside one of the old derelict buildings recently vacated by the ornithologists.

She used black plastic bin liners to set up a temporary dark-room in one of the lighthouse out-houses which had a sink and was wired for electricity. From out of their many rucksacks she pulled a small but adequate enlarger along with small bottles of fluids and chemicals.

There was something alchemical about the way she magicked up images that recorded our lives as they had been led a few days, a few hours ago.

And since they were both art students, and a few years older than me, I enjoyed their company. We would sit on the rocks near the jetty in the warm evenings and talk 'future plans'. The art school at Guildford sounded good. Close to London and all the galleries, yet close to the countryside and not too far distant from the sea. Over a year later I would apply to study there. I would be accepted. And very soon after, having finally chosen *exactly* the wrong time to give up smoking, I would have my hand on the door of a pub and decide not to go in. Less than an hour later it blew up. But that is another story with different, darker, poems.

Fire bombs in Dresden, Mackerel off Ailsa Craig

At last I found the metaphor for which I was searching. It was when Euan Linklater and Ross McGillivray went on leave and Jim Codey and Jack Starr replaced them that I finally understood. The lighthouse and the island, in fact all lighthouses and their islands or rocks, are like unchanging stage-sets for a play. Sometimes it is a comedy, sometimes a drama, occasionally a tragedy – but the props remain the same.

Each time the crew changed, so did the production, but not the stage-set. Suddenly I would find myself within a different play. It could be as light and fluffy as a TV sit-com with Terry Scott and June Whitfield, as dark as *Gormenghast*, or as adventurous as *The Treasure of the Sierra Madre*.

Euan and Ross were a little older than me, but not much. For my generation's Vietnam read their Korea. For Mick Jagger read Little Richard. For Moog Synthesiser, Fender Stratocaster. For Candy, Lolita . . . and so on.

But Jim Codey and Jack Starr were of another generation

entirely. They were both in their late fifties which meant that they were probably born in the early years of the First World War. Forget Candy and Lolita, we're talking Mata Hari and horse drawn carriages. Their youth was unemployment and the Jarrow Marches. Their manhood the next great war – in Jim Codey's case on submarines, in Jack Starr's the African desert.

With their presence, and their talk late into the night between watches, the lighthouse seemed to fill with memories, with scents from the Arab market and the sounds of distant gunfire. They had both been men of action, and had doubtless paid the price for some of those actions – remorse, disgust and sleepless nights. As Duncan on Pladda, who was even older yet seemed more innocent than these men, had said 'War is a nasty business, Peter. I hope you never see it.'

And the strange thing is they looked the part. It was as if Personnel at 84 George Street had phoned up central casting and said, 'We want someone who looks like Orson Welles to send to a lighthouse,' – that was Jim Codey. 'And while you're at it could you find someone who looks like Ernest Hemingway to accompany him?' – that was Jack Starr.

They were both big men. Jim Codey jumped ashore wrapped in a black oilskin. The peak of a battered captain's hat shaded his face and beard. But when he turned his head towards the sun he was Orson Welles' lost twin. Jack Starr wore a blue boiler suit and had a white hat pulled over his head like an inverted flower pot. He dressed like this for the whole time I knew him.

No time was wasted on niceties down at the jetty. It was straight back to the lighthouse and the lunch I had been preparing. This was a routine they had been through many hundreds of times.

I gathered these two men had worked together on other lights as well as Craigie, as I was learning to call it.

The three of us were to be together for a month. Although the sun shone constantly it was a dark, brooding period psychologically. Few words were spoken unless they had to be, or unless it was two in the morning.

Then something happened which bonded the three of us together. One afternoon Jim Codey had asked me to go out and help bring in the lobster creels. We left Jack in the kitchen preparing the evening meal.

Jim took the oars and I guided us towards the marker buoys. I can still remember the rich, sweet smell of pipe tobacco that seemed to seep through his skin. We had just reached the most distant creel where we would start to pull in the crayfish and their unwilling house companions the conger eels, when I looked over Jim's bull-broad shoulders and saw a huge wall of water blowing out from the side of the island. Behind me, at the other side of the island it was the same.

I later learned that Ailsa Craig is so high and wide that a strong gale can be blowing directly behind it yet the water in front will remain flat calm, completely sheltered by the mass of rock. That is what was happening to us.

'Time to batten down the hatches,' Jim boomed in his best submariner's voice. 'Leave the creels for tomorrow. We've got to get back before the wind veers.'

But he'd only rowed the length of a cricket pitch with two football fields still separating us from the distant jetty when the wind did indeed veer.

I saw it happening and felt its full force in my face at the same time. It was like being in a snow shaker rattled by an angry gorilla. The blue sky that had watched over our sheltered lagoon was washed aside by a thousand tones of grey as Gauguin became Turner and silver foam stippled against a torpedo black canvas.

I tasted salt on my lips and felt as if a fairground carousel had sheered off and was hurtling across empty space with us clinging to the sides.

Jim shouted at me across the narrow rowing boat as if his lungs were an industrial fan rattling in his chest. I only heard four words, words no one had ever said to me before, and they were, 'I need your help!' and realised that despite his efforts to pull us back to the shore we were still being blown out to sea.

I squeezed onto the narrow plank beside him and took an oar. Four-handed we pulled against the elements. The waves were so strong and the wind so fierce that at times we were suspended in mid-air, only to bang down a moment later on the cement-hard sea. I was afraid and excited at the same time. One tenth of my conscious brain realised with detached amusement that I was getting an erection. The other nine tenths concentrated every muscle on pulling at the oar. We were already far out on the open sea as Ailsa Craig herself was over ten miles from the mainland. Yet even at the heart of the storm there would be occasional split seconds of stillness when Jim would yell instructions in my ear. 'Forget about the jetty,' he cried. 'Make for shore anywhere. Pull hard! Pull hard!'

And then a giant wave would come crashing against us, enclosing the sky above us then dancing wildly on. Instinctively I knew that our lives depended on reaching any point of Ailsa Craig's shore before being blown totally past her and out to open sea.

For every ten feet we gained in one direction the storm would blow us back eight, and it was vital we keep that ratio. My arms ached and I was frightened I would lose my oar. We were now heading to the far side of the island when the miracle happened. The wind veered again, like a flautist readjusting a finger placement, and in the storm's momentary indecision the wind fell low enough and the mountain of sea flattened to a narrow path that led in to the shore. I could see a cave up ahead, steeple high and wide as a barn, and I aimed my energies at its dark centre. A thin apron of sand emerged between the rocky void and the liquid ocean. I can't remember how but we were up and running and pulling the boat behind us as if we'd trained for weeks to do just that.

Once again we had the mass of Ailsa Craig, like a giant mother ship, sheltering us from the storm. Everything seemed still and silent. And as I looked up towards the surrounding cliffs a big figure in blue overalls appeared to our right waving a white cloth hat.

'You were fucking lucky,' Jack Starr shouted as he jumped down beside us. 'There was a warning from the coastguard over the radio. Just ten minutes after you left. All boats to return to port. Gale force nine gusting to storm force.'

Jim Codey had found the pipe in his oilskin pocket and was clutching it tightly. Unlit.

'Aye, we were lucky alright. It took two of us to get her in.'

I was trying to roll a cigarette and noticed that my hands were shaking. The thin Rizla papers had remained dry throughout, although most of me was soaked through. My trainers were full of water and sand. 'I wasn't much use,' I said. 'You got us back.'

'Couldn't have on my own,' Jim insisted. 'There may not be much of you, but there was enough.'

'I didn't know whether to call the coastguard and tell them you were missing or to break into the emergency liquor in the medicine cabinet,' Jack told us. 'So I came looking for you instead. Left a message with Corsewall. Better get back and tell them you're ashore.' We pulled the boat up as high as we could and Jim said he'd come back once the storm had died down. The three of us trooped back to the lighthouse single file. Once out of our sheltered cove we were again hit by the full force of the wind and the rain which whipped against our faces and slashed hard against our legs below the knee.

But from that point onwards the three of us, but especially Jim Codey and myself, felt like comrades-in-arms. We'd fought a duel with the weather – no, we'd been ambushed by the weather while quietly going about our business of pulling food from the sea, and we'd managed to wriggle free.

It had been a Saturday afternoon the day Jim Codey and I went looking for lobster and found a storm. That evening, the dishes washed and stacked, the three of us gathered round the television set to watch *The Generation Game*. Bruce Forsyth, the game show host, had a catchphrase to suit every occasion and a miniskirted friend called Anthea Redfern who looked like a healthier, homelier version of Marianne Faithful.

It all seemed so cosy and domestic after the extremes of the afternoon. Jim Codey and Jack Starr roared with laughter at every innuendo and pratt fall. It turned out that they were also both great fans of the *Carry On* films. Big Jim Codey's favourite character was Kenneth Williams who in size, temperament and personality was the exact opposite of his greatest fan. Perhaps it was that thing of opposites attracting; the little old ladies fixed to their front row seats at wrestling matches.

And as for me, I was rediscovering television in a big way after two years of famine at art school. Watergate continued to be the hypnotic thread running through our lives injecting real, unscripted drama in between those fabricated in a studio. I enjoyed watching re-runs of Edward Woodward in *Callan*, with Russell Hunter as Lonely and Anthony Valentine as Toby Meres. There were all the old favourites from *Paul Temple* and *Pot Black* through to *The Two Ronnies* and *The Liver Birds*. If you were on an early watch the trick was to get the light going just after the hour or the half hour, even if it meant lighting it a little early. That way you missed the beginning rather than the end of most programmes. And there were a whole swag of programmes I'd never heard of, producing television stars I never knew existed. They had all begun since I first left home for art school. I met a Dutch detective called *Van der Valk*, a family of strange puppet-creatures called *The Wombles*, a drama called *Sutherland's Law* and a brand new comedy, *The Last of the Summer Wine*.

Often these programmes would be running in the background, especially in the afternoons if it was raining. As often as not I'd find myself a spot at the kitchen table with gouache and crayons and an expanse of white cartridge paper.

At such times Jim and Jack would treat themselves to 'a day at the races'. They did this in much the same way that the Professor on Pladda used to do his crossword puzzles. They would fold several days' newspapers at the racing pages. They could then study the form, discuss weather conditions and turf, and finally place their bets. There was an old monopoly set in the pantry cupboard. Most of the pieces were missing except the top hat and the battleship, but most of the money was there. They would divide this between them – and they couldn't have been more serious in intent had the toy money been real. They would happily spend two to three hours going through several days' races, then at the end of the afternoon, or sometimes from race to race, they checked the winners of each race in the next day's paper. They seemed to win about equally, and their emotions rose and fell as if the toy money had come straight from the Bank of Scotland.

*   *   *

There was a giant conger eel that lived under the jetty. Jim Codey's heart was set on catching it. 'It's got jaws as sharp as razors,' he told me one afternoon when we set out to lay the creels. 'Tough as a farmer's boot. It's the biggest and cleverest conger I've ever seen. It bit clean through a chain once that was hanging from the jetty. I've seen him a few times and he must be nine feet long.' It was a patient waiting game that Jim and the eel had been playing for years. It seemed neither wanted to die of old age with their battle unresolved. 'Got to respect that kind of cunning,' Jim said. 'That instinct for survival.' And he pushed us away from the jetty with the end of his oar.

Sometimes we went fishing together. Usually we would plan it the night before. But one afternoon while Jack was on duty Jim came rushing to get me, gripping a pair of binoculars in one hand. 'Quick!' he cried. 'Shoal of mackerel. I can see them close to shore. Get a couple of crates from the storeroom. I'll get the lines.'

In less than five minutes we were on the sea. In less than ten we were in the middle of a shoal of mackerel that must have stretched a quarter of a mile in every direction. It was a flat calm day yet the sea was frothing with their activity. Those at the top of the shoal constantly broke the surface water as a million eyes bobbed up and down like yo-yos. We didn't need any bait. Jim had special lines already prepared for such occasions. There were six hooks on each, two feet apart with a weight at the end. For fifteen minutes we threw our lines over the side of the rowing boat and then immediately hauled them back up with a silver darling flashing from each barb. It didn't take long to fill both crates, but Jim wanted to keep going so we then just threw them flipping and flapping into the bottom of the boat until the shoal had passed and the water rearranged itself into a mirror.

As soon as we got back we gutted them and stashed them in

the big freezer. Jack Starr was digging in the vegetable patch when we got back. 'Leave a few aside for me,' he shouted when he saw our catch. 'I've aye had a mind to try smoking mackerel.' And true to his word that afternoon he built a makeshift kiln from bricks and straw and placed one of the wire gratings from inside the oven on top of it. It was more like a barbecue, but the important thing is it worked. We re-arranged our evening meal around them and Bill served them up with a huge pot of mashed potato and peas, both of which had been home-grown in our sheltered garden.

'If I hadn't joined the lighthouse service, I would probably have become a prison officer,' Jim Codey told me one morning when I was starting a two o'clock Rembrandt. 'Might have been a governor by now,' he reflected. 'I was interviewed for both jobs about the same time. Peterhead Prison is where I would have worked, near Aberdeen. Furryboot City they call it,' but the joke, once again, was lost on me. 'It's a great city is Aberdeen. All the pubs sell stovies at lunchtime. I might make some next time I'm on lunches.' At that time of the night we all rambled on in a kind of free association, anything to keep our eyelids from closing over.

He'd already told me how he stayed in the military police for several years after the war, being posted to Aden, Germany, and finally Cyprus. 'It gives you discipline, being in a service,' he said. 'Although some of the younger men, with their trades unions and their working to rule wouldn't have lasted a week in a real war. You've got to be decisive. Know when to pull the trigger or stay your hand.' He pulled on his pipe and the room filled with sweet tobacco smoke.

Jim Codey was an enigma. He had the looks and the temperament of someone you would expect would be living a wild outdoor life, yet all the jobs he did, or aspired to – submarines, lighthouses, prisons – were about containment of some kind. Containment in an all-male world. I later learned he had, like most lighthouse keepers I knew, a very happy family life. He reminded me of a performance artist I met many years later who would, in a gallery setting, put his body through the most gruelling deprivations – sleep, food, mental stimulation – as he carried out a prescribed series of actions and inactions. Off duty, out of the white cube, he was a *bon viveur*, holidaying at exotic locations, dining well and partying even better.

In the dark watches beyond midnight when at its best your mind still felt it was being tumble-dried in a soup of tiredness, Jim would talk me round to consciousness with his memories of the war. He'd been part of a special unit of military police who were assigned to submarines. He seemed to have fond memories of his life under water, its confinement and the camaraderie that went with it. But his stories would always surface in the dark estuaries of bombed cities. Dresden especially with its hail of fire bombs and its sleet of phosphorous. 'People were being shot in the water,' he once said, distantly. 'Out of kindness. Their skin was on fire. They'd get below the water surface and the flames would go out. But as soon as they bobbed up again for air the phosphorous would re-ignite. All you could do was shoot them.'

Who was the 'you' in that last sentence? I often wondered but never asked. Did Jim Codey witness these things, did he go into a still smouldering city to create order, or did he hear about them second-hand?

Sex in the Bush

'How do you survive so long on a lighthouse without women?'
That's another of the questions most frequently asked of a lighthouse keeper, after the one about 'how did you get the job in the
first place?' No one would think to ask it of you ashore, in a city
or a village. Yet many young men and women – older ones too
I've heard – go for months and even years without sexual contact.
Young boys especially can travel from the ages of ten to twenty
without any physical contact with another human being what-
soever. No wonder many find it difficult to express their
emotions. And they've all been given this great gift which no one
talks about.

And so like the rest of the population, from the teenager in
her bed to the monk in his monastery, the sailor at sea or the
secretary with her head full of romance and Roses Chocolates,
lighthouse keepers please themselves from time to time, often
fantasising about mermaids in fishnet stockings.

But amongst ourselves, in the kitchen or in the light chamber,
or in the living quarters at two in the morning, all things sexual
were taboo. No one even told jokes with a sexual theme. Family

and children or ageing relatives were spoken of frequently with love and affection. But sex, or *hochmagandie* as Robert Burns called it, was never mentioned.

With one exception. Jack Starr. You couldn't get him to stop talking about it. *Especially* at two in the morning.

'Some women are quiet as mice when you're humping them, Peter my boy,' he began to soliloquise during the first change of watch I shared with him. It was one forty-five in the morning. 'Others scream like gulls, or moan like the wind on a frosty night. I knew one lassie who was widowed from a coastguard. She'd shout out the shipping forecast just before she peaked: Tyne! Forties! Fastnet! Tyne Dogger! Apparently he liked it that way. God, I've known some women. Fifteen years I spent in Australia, Peter my boy. God's own country. I visited every state, I worked the land, played in the cities and shagged the women. You'll never have heard possums going at it? Jesus, the noise they make would waken the dead. I knew a lass in Fremantle who sounded like a possum when she was goin' for it. Great place Fremantle, down on the Indian Ocean. I'd been up pearling in Broome, we're talking the dry season of, when was it, '53? No, I tell a lie it was '54, the year before I worked on the construction job for the Melbourne Olympics. I rented a room above a wee pub called The Hope and Anchor, 'till I moved in with a little Chinese lassie out in the boondocks. God she was a princess. Must have been a flute player in an earlier life the things she could do with her fingers. She sounded like a little bird when she came. Coo-ed like a dove so she did.'

'Stop it,' I used to say inwardly. 'Stop it,' once he got going. But he carried on just the same.

'Whereas Annie, Annie down in Fremantle, that's who I was going to tell you about before I got side-tracked, Annie purred like a contented kitten, when she wasn't screaming like a possum that is. You know, I drifted from job to job, but it was a good life. Was working in a pub in Fremantle, so I was . . . Annie was the landlord's daughter . . . hair as red as carrots, but that was the Irish in her. Then I crossed the Nullarbor when her father found out. He was Daft Eddie the landlord. He was a dangerous bugger was Daft Eddie. Kept a loaded gun under the counter. Still feared a Japanese invasion. I told him, Eddie I said, if the Japanese come you're onto an earner, but he wouldnae listen. Then he caught me an' Annie on the pool table one night after the pub shut, shaggin' like mongrels . . . that's when I did a runner.'

And so it went on. Every change of watch I spent with Jack he'd sit there in his blue boiler suit with his white cloth hat, chain-smoking Woodbines, and I'd listen to him relive his thirties and forties as he shagged his way from isolated mining settlement to harbour pub to single farms bigger than Wales where, if he's to be believed, he rode the boundaries repairing fences and forming on-off-on relationships with a string of aboriginal women from Broome through to Darwin and round the Top End to Cairns.

I know all this because he got out the atlas on one particular night and showed me his route.

'I teamed up with this fisherman in Cairns, Charlie Kalder was his name. He'd come down for the booze and the birds. Normally he worked up in the Gulf of Carpentaria, in little boats they called cockroaches. They'd ferry back and forth between Cape York and New Guinea, taking guns in and trading them for drugs. He was a good man was Charlie. Wouldn't have trusted him with my boots mind you, but good company all the same. They found him dead one morning. Stabbed seventeen times. His body was lying outside a toilet block, his head bashed in. The papers said it was the local kids and they arrested a few, but I reckon it was a drug deal gone wrong. Last time I saw him he'd been talking about returning to England. He came from Scarborough originally. Said he missed the frosty winter mornings. Once a year, on his birthday, his granny would send him a copy of the local newspaper. Always the issue on the 17th of February. I remember that. He'd read every word of it. The year I knew him he read about his sister's first child being born, like in the announcements section. There was a tear in his eye and he got very drunk that night. They buried him in the corner of a little cemetery on the outskirts of town. I put a little cairn of stones at the head of the grave, in the shade of a banana palm. Don't think he'd have wanted a cross. He was always talking about Lenin and had plans to catch a Blue Star freighter to the Caribbean and then on to Cuba. Said he had friends there who would see him right. Damn shame he died the way he did.'

I was twenty years old and I slowly felt, as the days turned into weeks that I was turning into an old man. It wasn't such a bad feeling, but strange. Every night I would hear Jim Codey reliving the fire-bombing of Dresden and looking ahead to his retirement. Four hours later Jim Starr would be back in the Australian bush re-inventing his past as he ricocheted around the great southern continent like a loose cannon. And in-between I would be up in the light chamber writing my novel, dreaming of the future, staring at the night sky and understanding why the ancients played join-the-dots with the constellations. Sometimes I would invent my own, leaning on the rail in a half-dream-like state, kept awake by the spray and the cold wind.

A little above the horizon was Rita the Meter Maid. Northeast of her was Westinghouse The Food Blender. Then, stretching halfway across the sky I baptised The Electric Guitar and could imagine Hendrix up there plucking it with his teeth and breathing new life into 'The Star-Spangled Banner' like a demented black Vishnu. Spinning high above the North Pole I named Cleo the Hot Water Bottle. Christ it was cold. I really wanted to hug somebody.

'Don't you want somebody to love? Don't you need somebody to love? Wouldn't you love somebody to love? You better find somebody to love.' The supply ship had arrived with mail from home, two tins of tobacco, and best of all new batteries for my giant cassette recorder. That's how I was able to play my tape of Grace Slick and the Great Society, the lyrics slopping around my head like soup in an old pot. *Don't you want somebody to love?* I was up in the light room surrounded by a whole week's worth of the *Scotsman* newspaper. I was starting to plan my much-postponed shore leave in earnest.

Originally I had been posted to Ailsa Craig for a month, which was a normal term of duty. Within a week of that time being up, a call had come through on the radio asking me if I would do another fortnight with Jim and Jack. I didn't have to, they stressed, and of course I agreed although I had to push away again all the normal things in life that had been so close to my grasp.

By the time the extra two weeks were up I had allowed myself to look forward to a walk down a High Street, a meeting with a friend, an impromptu meal, a rock concert, perhaps a meeting of flesh and naked warmth. Perfume of a night . . .

But then another call came. McTeague, the supernumerary who was meant to replace me, had been rushed to hospital with impacted wisdom teeth. Could I, wondered Donald Donaldson – it was him phoning in person this time – could I possibly manage another fortnight, we won't ask again? We've been getting very good reports about your progress, Peter. Could we even tempt you to think about taking the job on full time? Well, with all that flattery it would have been difficult to say no. So like a prisoner losing his remission for a second time I reluctantly agreed.

Jim and Jack must have realised the disappointment that I preferred not to voice, as I went about my duties like a good Stoic.

'It's a fine thing you're doing, son,' Jim told me. 'But if they ask again, tell them no. I've never done eight weeks straight on a light and I've been in the job over twenty years.'

'Don't want you turning into another Lachlan Fairbairn,' Jack put in his two bob's worth. 'Three months on Skerryvore without relief, and one of the other keepers dead on him.' But just the name Lachlan Fairbairn made me feel part of an expanded brotherhood. And that night, when Jim Codey belled me awake at 1.45 a.m., I asked him what Jack had meant.

'I take it you've heard of Lachlan,' Jim asked me.

'They were always talking about him on Pladda,' I replied. 'Sounds like quite a character.'

'Aye, he's that alright.'

'So what happened on Skerryvore?' I asked, pouring myself a cup of tea and cutting a lump of cheese to go on the bread that Jim had already sliced.

'Well, they say that's what turned him strange. Made him eccentric. But he was like that long before. I'm one of the few that know,' he added cryptically. 'But on Skerryvore he'd done an extra month like yourself, except it was the middle of winter and the storms were particularly bad that year. Then after eight weeks continuous Relief Day came, but no ship – it was all done by ship then – no ship arrived. Relief Plus One, Relief Plus Two, the days passed and the men had run out of tobacco. Eventually Relief Plus Four came and went and that meant of course the three of them had to do another four weeks – which would make twelve for Lachlan in total.

'Usually there is a big spare supply of tobacco for such eventualities, but for some reason no one had been re-ordering it. One of the three, Archie Fraser, was a really heavy smoker,' Jim continued, filling his own pipe. 'A Woodbine man like Jack, but a chain-smoker. He went to pieces after a few days. And remember Skerryvore comes straight out the sea, there was no escape for a solitary walk. No proper exercise to sweat it off. You were in the tower all day and all night. But the guy had other problems. His marriage was not happy. One of his children had died the previous year. And it was a year to the day of his kiddy's death that Lachlan found him hanging from the tower, like a second weight. They got the body down and they were able to radio to shore. But the waves were sixty feet high day after day. They couldn't even send a Sea King as there was no landing pad in those days.'

'So what did they do?' I asked, now wide awake and fixed on every word.

'They'd recently had a big freezer installed on Skerryvore,' Jim continued, but I'd already guessed the horrible truth. 'They put the body in there. Lachlan and Rinn, the other keeper, had to finish the month on their own which meant doing three watches each every twenty-four hours. That alone is enough to drive a man demented.'

I was now rolling my own cigarette and warily checking how much tobacco was left in my tin.

'But what really spooked old Lachlan – and remember he'd been on there nearly three months – what really spooked him was that every time they needed something from the freezer, which was one of those chest ones like a huge white coffin in itself, there would be Archie staring up at him through the frozen peas and turkey giblets.'

'And that's what turned him eccentric. I understand now.'

'No, but you don't,' Jim went on. 'That's what awebody says, especially the younger men who like to embroider a tale in its telling. But Lachlan was made of sterner stuff than that. There were bigger demons eating away at him. Lachlan was one of the great unsung heroes of the Second World War. But it was all undercover work. I've never found out myself what he did, but it was in the early days, I know that. He could speak not just fluent French but could exactly mimic each regional dialect. He was captured by the Gestapo in '41. And they say the only reason they didn't shoot him outright was they thought he had information about a super-bomb. I don't know how much of that is true,' Jim sucked his pipe reflectively. In the low glow from the fire, and with the other lights turned down he looked ever the *doppelganger* for Orson Welles – somewhere between *Citizen Kane* and *The Third Man*. I could almost imagine zither music drifting in from the dark sea outside.

'But you know, the little wizard got away,' he laughed. 'Made it to the Hook of Holland and then back to England. But he was never the same again. The physical scars healed but not the mental ones. That's why the service tolerates his eccentricities. And he's never let the light go out.' I instinctively checked my watch by the firelight. It would soon be time for me to wind the light. 'If it ever came to that he'd be pensioned off,' Jim continued. 'I haven't seen him for years. We did a spell together on the Chicken. We used to play chess together, and he always beat me. He never lost that facility. They say he would have been ranked a Grand master but he never could stand the competitions, he just played for the fun of it. Well, time for bed. I will wish you goodnight.'

Once Jim left the living quarters I gathered up my things. I took my cassette recorder, my new Grace Slick tape, my tin of tobacco and a whole pile of that week's *Scotsman* newspaper. With that afternoon's supply ship had come a new box of books from the mainland library. I'd only had time for a quick rummage through, in between cooking the evening meal – veal with a mushroom sauce and mixed vegetables, I see from my little yellow notebook.

The Edinburgh Festival had just begun and I was planning to catch the last week of it after completing my extra spell of duty. Up in the lightroom I performed my keeperly duties and then spread out consecutive days' *Scotsman*s in a neat circle on the floor of the light chamber. Again, I have to consult my notebooks to see what was on, and it comes as no surprise to see all the old favourites. There were several versions of *Waiting for Godot*; Peter Ustinov was producing a version of *Don Giovanni* which Conrad Wilson, the *Scotsman*'s critic with an eye on opera, hoped would be as good as his earlier *Magic Flute* in Hamburg; the Cambridge Footlights Review were doing their thing in Portobello, and of course Stephane Grappelli was scraping his fiddle at the Dominion. The only thing I really fancied seeing was a George Melly concert which I circled with a fat blue felt pen.

Reading through the listings, comparing the official festival with the fringe, I was beginning to feel like a student again, and less like an old man. I planned my route through Edinburgh. Listed the friends I would invite to different events. There would be exhibitions with Lincoln, if he was back from the Highlands; late night concerts with Keith; long talks in the pub with Stuart, and poetry readings to go to with Andy.

And if I cared to extend my Platonic relationship with Suzy, perhaps a night club or two. She had mentioned a friend . . .

Arabian Horse Times

YOUTH EVENTS

Be sure to visit the
Arabian Horse Times
NEWSROOM
in Tingley Coliseum
to pick up your copies of the
Arabian Horse Times,
Youth Yearbooks and
Arabian Horse Times
EXTRA.

Watch live interviews daily.

GROUP PHOTO
Friday, July 31
after the morning session.

YEARBOOK
SIGNING PARTY
Friday, July 31
at Bein Performance Stalls
5:30 p.m.

299 Johnson Ave., Suite 150
Waseca, MN 56093
800-248-4637 toll free
507-835-3204 phone
507-835-5138 fax
www.AHTimes.com

YOUTH
COVERAGE
in
OCTOBER
issue of
Arabian Horse Times

*Call today and ask
about our win ad
DISCOUNTS
in the
Youth Nationals
SHOW
COVERAGE.*

Light Without Flesh

As I write this there are no longer any manned lighthouses around the coast of Britain. No aspiring novelist is up in the light chamber doing his word count with pencil, mental arithmetic and youthful optimism. No human presence is there in case of emergency. No wise old men are teaching the young the 'routine' and the ways of the world. No Finlay Watchorn passing on his culinary skills or Jim Codey teaching a boy to row and set down lobster creels. It's a damn shame and it makes you want to cry.

Being a guide to mariners was the main reason for lighthouses existing. But in an alchemical way it also turned raw young boys into – not men, but fully rounded human beings, however flawed. We should have kept all the lights manned – with men *and* women, somehow – and every young person could go through a two-week training like I did on Pladda. Two weeks would be enough to re-invent society. The good people of Thailand often spend a month or two as monks in a monastery before pedalling off on the cycle of life. In my wilder moments I imagine the lighthouses performing such a duty. Sadly, it was not to be. Lighthouse keepers were the first victims of the unhappy marriage between globalisation and economic rationalism. Ours was the first profession ever to be made totally redundant.

So if you are a bank teller worried about your future, a bookseller, a university academic or a travel agent – be very afraid. What the men in suits have done to lighthouse keepers they are planning to do to you – *because it makes economic sense.* They will catch you in their internet, fillet you with platitudes, and lock you in the cold store of unemployment.

In the more Orwellian regions of my imagination I sometimes glimpse a future as depopulated and de-humanised as Ailsa Craig is now – and run with equal precision. Satellites send data. Clouds form and break over oceans. Fog signals blow on cue, but there are no mariners to warn. The lighthouse flashes, the runway lights come on at dusk . . . traffic lights change to amber to green and back to red, but there is no one left to run a red light . . .

At various times of the night and day – sometimes around the breakfast table over our kippers and poached egg, sometimes with tea and cheddar during a long Rembrandt, we would debate the many-sided problem of who exactly would be the last lighthouse keeper. On the face of it you would think it would be the last man to be made redundant and finally close the door on the last manned light. But the problem was more complex than that because the lights would still need servicing by engineers. Perhaps they would be the last lighthouse keepers.

During my time on the lights the chief electrical engineer was as legendary as Lachlan Fairbairn. He was always dropping in unannounced with his massive toolbox, his pyjamas and his toothbrush. He spent three days on Ailsa Craig when I was there. And I can honestly say that fewer things worked when he left the island than when he had arrived for the annual check-up.

In looks – and probably in eccentricities – he resembled the middle-aged Wittgenstein, the nomadic Viennese philosopher. There is an edition of his brilliantly flawed *Remarks on Colour* in which his head and shoulders are silhouetted in black against a lipstick-red background. We're talking *doppelgangers* here and the likeness was uncanny. I can't remember his real name but the other keepers just referred to him as 'Einstein'. He had a portable radio with him which was about the size of a small safe and which he would strap to his back and climb with to the top of Ailsa Craig. God knows what he did up there, but one day he came back and claimed to have been talking to British troops in Northern Ireland.

It was just after Einstein left us that I got my first real taste of the fog signal. I'd heard tales of course but nothing quite prepared me for the *painfully* loud noise it made and the hours, turning into days, that it might have to blow.

Jim Codey showed me what looked like several sets of old-fashioned stereo headphones in the living-room cupboard.

'These are what 84 issued us with a few years ago. Utterly hopeless. We're supposed to wear them in bed when the fog signal's blowing. I tried it once and I nearly broke my neck when I rolled over in my sleep. So we just keep them in here, unwrapped and unused.'

He was about to show me how to switch on the horns. We walked across the cobbled forecourt to the radio room and the whole process really was as simple as switching on an electric light. We'd never had to use the fog horn while I was on Pladda, but I'd been taught what to do and it was a task of epic proportions involving turning what seemed like hundreds of dials – some half on, others full or a quarter turn. It was literally a twenty foot long, steam driven, Tibetan horn that sounded like the death rattle of an elephant.

On Ailsa Craig, by contrast, there was a neat bank of some forty horns mounted on a gantry. And here's the crazy part. On such a huge island with no shortage of distant nooks and crannies, it had been installed directly outside our living-room window.

The noise was fearsome. The good people of Girvan, over ten miles away, used to complain about the noise it made when it was blowing. Think what it was like at a couple of yards' distance! Imagine being grid-locked in a traffic jam and everyone blows their horn in unison at fifteen second intervals. Now magnify the volume by a factor of one hundred. It really was a physical pain one experienced.

On that occasion it blew for eighteen hours, but I heard horror stories that summer of the fog settling in for several days.

For me, it was a bit of a novelty. Until lunchtime certainly. Then it began to wear a bit thin. The three of us spent the afternoon indoors and I soon learned there was an art to holding conversations while the horn was blowing. Every fog horn, like every light, had its own signal. On Ailsa Craig it was a fairly simple one. One five second blast every fifteen seconds. And that was exactly how we divided up our conversations. Jim and Jack were used to it and fell into the routine easily.

Each of us would speak in turn for fifteen seconds and the conversation always revolved in a clockwise direction. It was a very democratic way of communicating, and if it was not for the awful noise in-between I would thoroughly recommend it.

It meant you had to plan what you were going to say in advance and hone down your conversation to fifteen second bursts. Of course, many hours later, when we had been speaking like this for almost a day and a night, we continued to do so and our staccato talk was punctuated by five seconds of glorious silence.

Anyway, the three of us sat in the living room all afternoon with a bottomless pot of tea and several packets of sweet digestives. We tried playing cards for a while, starting with five card poker and ending with pontoon, but the effort of concentrating on the game and the rhythm of the fog signal at the same time killed the pleasure of it.

Occasionally we'd go out and peer over the lighthouse wall, but we never could see even as far as the water. If there were any ships out there they'd be glad of our horn, no matter how much we cursed it.

Back inside I must have asked a question about the Irish navvies who had worked the quarry on Ailsa Craig, for soon I was being regaled at fifteen second intervals with tales of their bravado.

'Quite fucking fearless,' Jack said from his armchair, his white hat pulled down to his eyebrows. 'It was as if they didn't feel pain at all.'

BLAAAAAAAST!!!

'Aye, they had their accidents,' Jim grasped the conversational baton. 'I remember one day Finbar the foreman appeared in the kitchen, clutching his tackle. Blood just pouring down between his legs.'

BLAAAAAAAST!!!

'Look, I know I've got my fifteen seconds,' I addressed them both. 'But just carry on without me till I get the hang of this.'

BLAAAAAAAST!!!

'Och, you'll get used to it son,' Jack told me. 'Just butt in when you think o' something to say. Now where were you Jim?

BLAAAAAAAST!!!

'"Have you got a darning needle?" asks Finbar, cool as a choc-ice at a Saturday matinee. "I just need to put in a few wee tucks."'

BLAAAAAAAST!!!

'I'm going to top up the tea,' I said. 'You two just carry on.'

BLAAAAAAAST!!!

'Och, they were wild times,' Jack continued. 'Do you remember

Ben Gunn? Was he still living here when you came to Craigie, Jim?'

BLAAAAAAAST!!!

'So I told him, "We need to get you to hospital," there was blood dripping all over the lino. But he looked at me as if I'd called him a pansy. "Just get us a sail-maker's needle and a bit of twine," he insisted.'

BLAAAAAAAST!!!

'You're pulling my leg,' I accused Jim, pouring out mugfuls of tea all round. 'So what happened, anyway?'

BLAAAAAAAST!!!

'Ben Gunn lived in the closest house to the light,' Jack took up his own story, lighting up a Woodbine and shaking out the match slowly like a doctor with a thermometer. 'Even after all the others had gone, he stayed on. Just him and the donkey.'

BLAAAAAAAST!!!

'It's all true,' Jim insisted, but there was a twinkle in his submariner's eye. 'The last I saw of him was his massive bulk disappearing into the setting sun, back towards the quarry. He was clutching his wedding tackle in one hand and trailing a long length of thread in the other.'

BLAAAAAAAST!!!

'Donkey?' I asked incredulously. 'I've never heard of a donkey before. How did it get here?'

BLAAAAAAAST!!!

'It came with the quarrymen. Until they got the wee railway built it used to help pull the stone back to the jetty.'

BLAAAAAAAST!!!

'I heard later that one of his mates knocked Finbar out with a punch after giving him a quarter bottle of Bell's. All bush hospital stuff. Then they got to with the needle and the anti-septic and stitched him up like a sail.'

BLAAAAAAAST!!!

'Ben hated that donkey. Every morning it was the same pantomime. The animal would start braying at six o'clock on the dot. Then if you were on duty you'd see wee Ben Gunn in his nightshirt hurling rocks at it, chasing it off to the beach.'

BLAAAAAAAST!!!

I felt like I wanted to split in two. It was a truly Borghesian moment and the paths were forking before my ears. 'So was he ok when he came round?' I quickly asked Jim. 'And what happened to Ben?' I demanded of Jack before the fog signal got its word in edgeways.

BLAAAAAAAST!!!

'Och, Ben still lives on the island,' Jack said to my astonishment. 'In a cave on the west beach. He eats only dandelions and seaweed.'

BLAAAAAAAST!!!

'Don't you believe him, Peter,' Jim said, and I've never felt so disappointed in my life. 'He died not long after he killed the donkey.' At least our paths were converging again.

BLAAAAAAAST!!!

'He killed the donkey? Why did he do that? And what happened to him, how did he die?' I heard a note of urgency in my voice.

BLAAAAAAAST!!!

'It was right out of order,' Jim continued. 'He took his sledge hammer to the donkey one morning. A single blow to the skull. I saw it but it was too late to stop it. The creature just buckled at the . . .'

BLAAAAAAAST!!!

'When I caught up with Finbar the next day he was right as rain. But walking with a bit of a limp. We had words later though. They were always messing about with dynamite and Finbar was the worst of them.'

BLAAAAAAAST!!!

I'd been shuffling the playing cards at the table during the five second blasts of the horn. I started to deal myself a hand of patience.

'So what about Ben Gunn? How did he die?' I turned over the eight of clubs.

BLAAAAAAAST!!!

'Old age, poor diet, loneliness. Who knows? Perhaps remorse for the donkey,' Jack said philosophically. 'We didn't find him for days.'

BLAAAAAAAST!!!

'I caught him trying to lob a stick of dynamite at a basking shark. Well out of order. "Finbar," I said, "You're a fucking . . ."'

BLAAAAAAAST!!!

'It was wee Jimmy Meadows who found him. Thank God I wasn't on duty. Jimmy left the service not long after that. They say he still just sits in a chair and stares out the window all day.'

BLAAAAAAAST!!!

I turned over the Jack of Hearts. 'So how many quarrymen were there? And what happened to the bodies? I mean the donkey and Ben Gunn?'

BLAAAAAAAST!!!

'Must have been about twenty of them at the peak of employment. Blew up their houses, the lunatics, with the remains of the explosives. Fine wee cottages they were too.'

BLAAAAAAAST!!!

'It was the rats that caused the mess. Wee Jimmy came out with his face as white as flour. You see there were rat holes all round the cottage Ben lived in. And Ben had his own unique solution. They say he'd been a fine engineer before he went troppo.'

BLAAAAAAAST!!!

Two of diamonds. I didn't have anything to say. King of clubs. We enjoyed the silence.

BLAAAAAAAST!!!

'He wasn't Irish himself,' Jim supplied a point of information. 'Went to a good school in Dorset. Then in the war, the Burmese Railway, he came back a bag of skin and bones. That's what Finbar told . . .'

BLAAAAAAAST!!!

'Anyhow,' Jack's face carried a look of amusement and I hated to think what was coming next. 'Ben's party trick was to hacksaw three slits around the rat holes. One at the top and two at the sides. He was mad as a meat axe.'

BLAAAAAAAST!!!

Four of clubs . . . Five of clubs . . . Queen of diamonds . . . Ace of spades.

BLAAAAAAAST!!!

'He went to live with a cousin in Donegal. But even then he was living like a hermit. Then his cousin got him a job at the local quarry, and when it went to the wall the job on Craigie came up and most of the quarrymen transferred here.'

BLAAAAAAAST!!!

I seemed to remember The Beatles had once been called The Quarrymen. Then Johnnie and the Moondogs.

'Once he'd done that he stuck razor blades in the slits. And when the rats ran through the holes they were sliced to ribbons. Wee Jimmy reckons they kept running up the walls and over the bed. He said there was blood everywhere and Ben lying there in state . . .'

BLAAAAAAAST!!!

I felt sick. I gathered the cards up and gave them a good shuffle.

BLAAAAAAAST!!!

'Nasty business, war,' Jim Codey reflected. 'Took me a long time to get over what I saw in Dresden. The allies bombed it flat. God knows how anyone survived. But they were there, crawling over the rubble like ants.'

BLAAAAAAAST!!!

'In the finish the local police from Girvan came out with forensics. Took all his stuff away in plastic bags and sent the body back to Ireland. Then they fumigated the cottage. Sent two guys dressed like astronauts.'

BLAAAAAAAST!!!

'And what about the donkey?' I wondered. Seven of hearts. Six of clubs.

BLAAAAAAAST!!!

'The donkey's buried over near the cottage, marked with a few thistles and a pile of granite,' Jim concluded both stories with a suck on his pipe. 'And Ben Gunn's found peace at last. He's gone to the big hermit's cave in the sky.'

BLAAAAAAAST!!!

That night was the only time that our four-hourly watches went askew. I tried to go to sleep about nine that evening until it was my turn to start work at two. Jim Codey woke me up, and when I staggered into the darkness to make my way to the living room, I bumped into Jack Starr stumbling through the dark. His sleep patterns had been skewed by the constant braying of the horns. Jim told him to go back to bed and get another four hours' sleep in, while I prepared for a very noisy watch. I spent most of it in the tower with The Incredible String Band's *Changing Horses* turned up to full volume. I paced around the light chamber wondering when the fog would finally clear.

Next morning, to the relief of us all, it was a perfect day. The mainland shimmered on the horizon through a gentle heat haze.

Shore Leave II:
The Edinburgh Festival

Leaving Ailsa Craig was easier than leaving Pladda. Jim Codey and I left together. Jack Starr was having to stay on an extra fortnight. We made the journey in silence. As The Craig grew smaller behind us, the mainland loomed larger.

Jim took me to his house in Girvan for lunch. It was strange seeing him in a domestic setting surrounded by his wife Betty and teenage daughters.

Afterwards we went to a harbourside pub where we each had a pint of Tartan Special.

By mid-afternoon I was back in Glasgow. It was great to be surrounded by family and friends, but the big question of 'the future' hung like a forming cloud in an otherwise blue sky. Somehow at the age of twenty dropping life to hitch-hike to India didn't seem as appealing an idea as it had three years earlier. And besides, part of me still felt like a late middle-aged man after my routine on Ailsa Craig with Jim and Jack.

That night, down the Rubaiyat in Byres Road, I caught up

with Keith, Stuart and Dave. Where conversation over the past eight weeks had as likely been about Rommel, Montgomery and Churchill, now I was firmly back in the present.

'Did you see Nixon's got the audacity, the sheer gall,' Stuart was saying, 'to throw a White House party for returning GIs?'

'And one *Playboy* bunny,' Keith added.

'Bob Hope cheering on the troops.'

I'd caught the scene myself. John Wayne and Sammy Davis Jr had been working the lawn as well. Little Henry Kissinger the big hero, flocked on all sides by returning servicemen's wives.

'They even gave him a fucking plaque "Richard the Lionhearted",' Dave said with complete disillusionment, and wisely turned the talk round to real heroes.

'Have you played *Hot Rats* yet?' he asked Keith. 'The Captain's vocals are amazing.'

And soon we were off down the long and winding road of rock music and literature.

I sipped my pint and read the etched mirror opposite:

> Here with a Loaf of Bread
> beneath the Bough,
> A Flask of Wine, a Book
> of Verse – and Thou
> Beside me singing in
> the wilderness –
> And Wilderness is Paradise
> enow.

The pub was packed and our group later expanded with the arrival of Sarah and Jean and Arthur and Effie. The noise level rose and we drifted from an open table discussion into talking amongst twos and threes.

Keith was telling me about the long-shot possibility of The Grateful Dead playing somewhere near Pitlochry at the autumn equinox. I hoped for him it was true. His whole record collection, not to mention his wardrobe, was centred around the Dead.

Most of us had parted company with higher education that summer, one way or another, and while I was working the lights Keith had secured a driving job delivering orthopaedic chairs to some of the most remote parts of Scotland.

'Do you fancy coming along for the ride?' he asked me. 'I've got to take one to Fort William tomorrow. Then the next couple of days its Ingliston racetrack just outside Edinburgh. That's not till the evening. They're setting up a special booth for the weekend races.' And he attempted to answer the question I was wondering, 'Maybe drivers get a lot of back pain, I dunno.'

'You're on,' I said enthusiastically, 'especially if we can take in a couple of acts at the festival.'

Keith lived with his parents in a big house off Great Western Road. It was divided in two and the other half was occupied by the sculptor Benno Schotz. The garden was full of heroic figures hewn from stone.

The next morning I walked round to Keith's from my Mum and Dad's place. The van was already parked in the driveway and loaded with the one chair we had to take to Fort William. I had slept longer the previous night than I had for over two months, although I did leap out of bed at two in the morning ready to go on watch.

Walking through the railway station at Hyndland and up Novar Drive it felt really strange not to be surrounded by water. It was probably an ordinary, quiet day but there seemed to be people everywhere. I had re-entered the atmosphere. The gannet had landed.

We used the journey north to plan what we would do in

Edinburgh the next day. I had a copy of the Fringe programme and Keith had *Live Dead* playing on a portable cassette recorder.

This album is to Dead Heads what the Holy Grail was to the Crusade. For the next six hours it was all we listened to. We passed through Alexandria and along the side of Loch Lomond accompanied by 'Dark Star'. Between Arrocher and Crianlarich we were totally absorbed in 'Saint Stephen' and 'The Eleven'. Rain was lashing the windscreen when we stopped in Bridge of Orchy for a bridie and some tomato soup out of white polystyrene cups, but we were happily engrossed in 'Turn On Your Love Light'.

And so it went on until we arrived in Fort William to 'Death Don't Have No Mercy'.

During this time, and on the long journey back – it was a hell of a distance to go to deliver a vibrating chair, when you think of it – we picked out a few gems for the morrow. Roger McGough and Brian Patten were giving a reading somewhere down in the Grassmarket. Ivor Cutler was in a church hall at the top of Market Street, and there was a nude Swedish version of *Waiting for Godot* intriguingly played by an all female cast. I put a big tick next to that one and wondered what the chances were of getting backstage after the performance. We decided to give Peter Ustinov a miss.

The next day, bright and early, we loaded the van up with brochures and a collapsible exhibition stand as well as three types of chairs and footstools. Keith told me there was a company song that was even louder than the company tie which featured reclining chairs in a half drop repeat. The parent company was based in America and the whole sales pitch was driven by mid-Atlantic jargon. We stopped at Byres Road to pick up copies of the *Scotsman* and the *Glasgow Herald*. Keith had selected *Workingman's Dead* and

American Beauty for our pleasure that day and we beetled along the motorway linking Glasgow with its old rival Edinburgh to the strains of 'Uncle John's Band' and 'Dire Wolf'. We were there in just over an hour. We managed to park the van down the back of Princes Street in Cambridge Street and like all Glaswegians in Edinburgh headed straight for Rose Street which in those days was like a cross between Carnaby Street and a brewery.

The sun was out, and mini-skirts and denim had been the items of choice selected from the wardrobes of the young east coast girls and their home counties counterparts up for the festival. I'd struck a deal with Keith that we'd split for three hours while he trawled the record shops for boot-leg Dead albums and I did my annual round of the art galleries. I was quite catholic in my tastes which ranged from home grown talent at the New 57 Gallery to Richard Demarco's trail-blazing art events in Charlotte Square (I think it was Dan Flavin's light works that year) to the more staid Royal Scottish Academy and National Gallery on the Mound. I agreed to meet Keith outside the Scottish National Portrait Gallery where Sandy Moffatt had a solo exhibition, splitting the difference between Leith Walk and Princes Street.

From there we repaired to Milnes Bar for a well-earned pint. Two years and a million lifetimes ago I had a brief, teenage, fumblingly clumsy but ego-boostingly brilliant relationship with an English student I'd met at a Procol Harum concert at Stirling University. She'd gone there from Edinburgh, I'd travelled down from Dundee. We'd met at a Pete Brown poetry reading before the concert. Our lips met a split second before our John Lennon granny glasses locked horns with each other.

She was into Dylan Thomas and Neil Munro. To her the Liverpool poets were lightweight and the Beat poets chauvinist pigs. Come to think of it we had more in common in our taste for beer. She lived in a tiny attic room above Rose Street and first introduced me to Milnes Bar which is also known as The Poet's Bar. It's not in Rose Street itself but just round the corner in Hanover Street, a conte stick's throw from the Royal Scottish Academy and down a wee flight of stone steps. In those days it was anonymous enough to be missed by most of the tourists and festival-goers. Here all the great Scottish poets of the twentieth century gathered to talk and drink and plan their linguistic revolutions. Sandy Moffat painted them all.

One poem by Louis Macneice captures the spirit of the place, the city, the pub, the nation. 'Bagpipe Music', populated by ladies whose 'knickers are made of crepe-de-chine, their shoes are made of python, Their halls are lined with tiger rugs and their walls with heads of bison.'

Someone once described Edinburgh during the three weeks of the festival as being the Athens of the North, but qualified it by saying that for the other forty-nine weeks of the year it reverted to being the Reykjavik of the South. No matter, the place was jumping when we arrived. The traffic was held up while a pipe band meandered across the road to Princes Street Gardens. Japanese tourists buckled under the weight of their camera gear, as ice cream vendors vied with hot dog stalls to see who could draw the biggest queue and create the most havoc. I felt good. I felt young again. And as we drove round Charlotte Square, now home of the book festival, I realised we were about to enter George Street, headquarters of my current employers, the esteemed Commissioners of the Northern Lights. And sure enough there was No 84 with the virgin white lighthouse above the lintel. I immediately thought 'tea and biscuits'.

I wanted to tell Keith what it was like. I tried to, and he understood some of it. But it was another world – not necessarily of the past . . . just different.

The rest of that day and night blurs into two dozen other Edinburgh festivals that I have attended. My abiding memory is of returning to Glasgow via the Ingliston racetrack. A security guard let us in around midnight and we off-loaded our cargo. Before leaving we did several circuits of the track to the accompaniment of *American Beauty* which some regard as the classic Dead album: 'Truckin', 'Sugar Magnolia', 'Friend of the Devil', and the utterly haunting 'Box of Rain'.

'How's your novel going?' Lincoln asked me when we met up in Dundee the following week. We were back in our Perth Road curry house to which we'd repaired after a pint in the Tav.

'It's getting there,' I replied. 'I've been trying to average two thousand words on every watch. But I've never written anything this long before. Maybe I'll stick to short stories. I'm not sure how you deal with the fact that your own mood changes over many months of writing but perhaps you are trying to sustain the same mood throughout the novel. It's a tricky one.'

Lincoln had already filled me in on his time in the Highlands, up in the far north-east. He painted a picture of sloping rain and bracken, his shoulders hunched under the weight of a dead deer shot by wealthy English tourists. A nip of whisky and a pair of lungs full of fresh air. His own painting was looking good too; oils painted *al fresco* on various sizes of canvas.

'But I've got this idea for a TV series about a lighthouse keeper detective,' I took a mouthful of lager to wash down the chicken tikka. 'A touch of the Sherlock Holmes, you see. He likes his solitude and withdraws to the lighthouse every other month to work on his different cases. Then he plunges back into life every other month when he gets shore leave – London, Vienna, San Francisco – solving crimes as he goes.'

'The opium dens and brothels of Europe,' Lincoln entered

into the spirit of my ramblings, 'where crown princes mix with Disney executives. Maybe you could make him an artist, Pete. Surveillance disguised as drawing.'

'I'm not sure who should play Watson or Bertie Wooster to his Holmes or Jeeves figure?' I mused. 'It could be one of the other keepers and they could have all their meaningful dialogue on the light. Or it could be someone on the mainland. A woman. Yes, I fancy a woman. . .'

I spent the rest of that week packing up my bedsit in Greenfield House. Different cardboard boxes would be stored by family and friends. The future was a totally unknown quantity. But at least my bank balance was healthy. There was a whole summer's wages sitting there untouched. I couldn't have spent more than five pounds over the last two months.

I decided to buy a camera. It was one of the best purchases I've ever made. It was a tiny Rollei camera, a miniature one with a collapsible lens that clicked open and shut. It came in a soft leather case and the whole thing could easily slip into the front pocket of my jeans. There was a built-in light meter next to the shutter and the flash which I bought separately was actually bigger than the camera. It was like something out of a James Bond movie, a parting present to Bond from the elderly boffin down in the basement of MI5. What was he called? Q, that was it.

'Wait till Felix Leiter sees that,' James drawls in his best Sean Connery brogue. 'I'll bring you back a photo of his face.'

It suddenly occurred to me that I better give 84 George Street my parents' address in Glasgow so they could contact me about any new posting. I phoned them up and was rather disappointed not to hear the friendly Liverpool accent of Rosie at the other end. There was a rather cold female with a sort of down-at-heel Morningside tone. It could even be the voice of the Kirk, or at least the minister's housekeeper.

'Thank you for informing us of your change in circumstances,' she said, as if in response to me telling her that I was out on parole and had just found lodgings that accepted ex-cons. 'Let me just check that no missives have been dispatched in the meantime. Please hold the line.'

I was in a coin box on Perth Road and feeding it like it had just come off a diet.

I was down to my last 10p when she returned.

'It is just as well I checked.' Yes, get on with it I cursed. 'You are to go to Highsker . . .'

Click. Purr. Purr. Purr.

'Hang on a minute!' I cried helplessly. 'Hang on. . .' but we'd been cut off.

'Highsker,' I said to myself, wondering how to spell it. 'I'm sure she said Hyskeir. Never heard of it.' I repeated the name to myself all the way along Perth Road. Damn it, I remembered, I'd packed my only atlas. I was about to go to the corner shop for change and call her back when I saw that the art school library was open. They'd have one, sure to.

The Times Atlas of the World – it would be there or nowhere.

I started looking under High . . .

Higgins Bay . . . High Wycombe . . . Hijaz . . . Hikurange . . . but no Highsker.

Then I thought it might begin Hy . . .

Hyde Park . . . Hyderabad . . . Hyland . . . Hyltebruk . . .

The librarian changed a ten shilling note for me and within minutes I was back out on Perth Road chatting to the ice maiden's frostier elder sister.

'Sorry, we were cut off,' I began, running my fingers along the neat pile of ten pence pieces I had deposited on top of the phone. 'I was phoning to . . .'

'Yes, yes, I know,' she hissed. 'You've to go to Hyskeir in the Hebrides . . .'

'Could you spell that please?'

'Do they teach you nothing in school. H.E.B.R.I . . .'

'No, the other place,' I rammed in more coins.

'You spell it H.Y.S.K.E.I.R. There is a letter for you in the post, you shouldn't be wasting my time with . . .'

'Thank you,' I hung up. Hope your roof leaks. The Hebrides, I mouthed aloud. The Hebrides, now that's somewhere I've never been before. I mooched along to the Deep Sea Fish Restaurant at the city end of Perth Road. Over a battered haddock and chips I slurped my tea and wondered how I could find out more. Perhaps the letter would come in the post tomorrow. I hoped so, as I was leaving Dundee the day after. Heading back to Glasgow. I remembered there was a specialist bookshop in Union Street that had a map department. It was late afternoon but they should still be open.

Dundee is a very livable city with no need for an underground or even an overground local rail system. You can walk everywhere, then you can turn round and walk back.

Within minutes I was in a cramped attic room, the air heavy with dust and particles of old parchment. Carefully I unfolded the touring map marked Hebrides, Outer and Inner, which were the only two aspects I knew about the place. Or the places.

There are over five hundred islands off the West Coast of Scotland. Some of them are much bigger than the Isle of Wight. Others are tiny rocks. I had an ominous feeling I was heading for the latter. I didn't bother with the index, I just scanned across the map keeping one eye on the shop assistant who was keeping both eyes on me.

My gaze rose from South Uist to North Uist, then on to Harris and Lewis and across to the Summer Isles and back down to Rum, Eigg, and Muck. To the south was Coll, Tiree and Mull, but that was way too far south in the near tropical waters lapped by the Gulf Stream. I started a slower circuit of the islands again, beginning at Barra but going anti-clockwise this time . . . and there it was. Halfway between Barra and Rum was the word Hyskeir, but I could see no island. It was that small. Then I realised that the 'i' of Hyskeir had two dots above it, and the smaller of them was to be my new home.

HYSKEIR

The Seaman's Mission,
Oban – The Whirleybirds

When my instructions for duty arrived the next day at Greenfield House I was surrounded by cardboard boxes and old suitcases containing clothes, books, and LPs.

Lincoln helped me carry them down to the hall and shouted up to tell me that a letter had just dropped through the letter box along with sundry bills and DHSS cheques for my fellow art students.

It informed me that in ten days' time I would be expected to travel to Glasgow and from there catch a train up to Oban where I was to stay one night at the Seaman's Mission.

In the morning a helicopter – I could scarcely believe it, a helicopter, and me who had never even flown before in a regular plane – a helicopter would take me to Hyskeir where my term of duty was expected to be of two weeks' duration. A mere bagatelle, I thought, compared to eight weeks on the Craig. But a helicopter . . .

*   *   *

Oban lies north-west of Glasgow and the train journey then took about three and a half glorious hours. The carriage was full of late-summer backpackers and pensioners on day trips – all packed lunches and thermos flasks. The city quickly turned into universal suburbs with their greenhouses, washing lines and garden sheds. Then came the little coastal towns of Dumbarton and Helensburgh, birthplace of David Byrne from Talking Heads. Soon we were rising above the banks of Loch Long and Garelochead, home to the American Polaris submarines which in the Cold War meant Glasgow would be one of the first cities 'taken out'. The upper reaches of Loch Lomond brought us eventually to Crianlarich where we stopped for twenty minutes for refreshments on the platform, the engine driver chatting to the local postman while three American backpackers practised Tai Chi next to the ticket office. We scared some deer at the edge of Rannoch Moor where the bare hills slope northwards to Ben Nevis in a patchwork of mottled browns and faded yellows rising finally to slate-grey and ice-white.

The Glasgow train all but rolls into the Oban sea, and when I inquired about where I could find the Seaman's Mission I was told it was just around the corner.

The Seaman's Mission, as I recall it, was more of a concrete all-male down-market guest house in which rooms and walls were called galleys, bulkheads, and cabins. To me, dressed in the uniform of a young hippy, it appeared to be full of Captain Birdseye lookalikes in yellow sou'westers and gumboots. They sat in faded armchairs listening to the shipping news and playing dominoes. They smoked every variety of pipe, cigarette and cigar imaginable, sometimes simultaneously. Both the architecture and the ambience gave the feeling of being in a very large ferry becalmed at sea, possibly in the crew's recreational quarters.

I walked slowly around the town centre – it doesn't take long

– and admired McCaig's Folly from below. It comes as a bit of a surprise to unwitting tourists to find a replica of the Colosseum in Rome towering above a West of Scotland fishing port, but it is there as a result of one of Britain's first job creation schemes in the late nineteenth century and the vanity of the McCaig family. At its foot lies Scotland's only inner-city distillery and spreading around that a multitude of hotels and bed and breakfast establishments still trading on Oban's Victorian reputation of being 'the Charing Cross of the Highlands'.

For a moment I swithered between having my evening meal in one of these establishments or in a pub, and in a trice I was in a harbourside hostelry ordering up crumbed haddock and a pint of export. The bar was noisy and smoky and full of good banter and laughter. Even the fruit machine by the snug was laughing money.

I felt good, and was looking forward to my next adventure.

Two days earlier I'd come across a gem of a poetry book in a second-hand shop in Glasgow that's called Voltaire and Rousseau, up near the university. It was a long narrative poem called 'The Wild Party' by Joseph Moncure March who I'd never heard of before or since. The sleeve notes described it as 'a hard-boiled, jazz-age tragedy told in syncopated rhyming couplets.' I'd been saving it up for just such a moment. I was soon lost in the story of Queenie and Burrs. I kept the book open with my right elbow while going for the haddock and chips with my left fork. The sky was darkening outside and I wondered between mouthfuls and verses what my surroundings would be like tomorrow night? Who would be my companions? I treated myself to a fine single malt, and wondered.

In a nook near the fireplace a fiddler was playing a slow strathspey. Two fishermen up at the bar argued in Gaelic. The only words I recognised were Rangers and Celtic.

With a warm glow in my heart I headed back to the Seaman's Mission for what I was sure would be a good night's sleep.

Half a dozen elderly seamen were clustered around the television set when I returned like a cross between a rugby scrum and a giant sou'wester. Even before I saw the screen I recognised the voices of Ken Barlow and Elsie Tanner. The highs and lows of life in a fictional suburb of Manchester was what drew these men who risked their lives on the high seas around the TV set. I stood at the back of the room for a few minutes, mesmerised by the north of England tapestry unravelling before me, as Percy Sugden snooped on Curly Watts and Vera Duckworth gave husband Jack a right tongue-lashing in front of Bet Lynch at the Rover's Return.

And so I sloped off to bed.

There're a lot of songs about waking up in the morning, from hard blues to soft romantic numbers. Was it The Move who sang:

> Woke up this morning half asleep
> With all my blankets in a heap
> And yellow roses scattered all around me . . . ?

Anyway, there were no roses just a few faded bluebells on the thin eiderdown, and I had had a fairly fitful night's sleep. Several times I had been woken by drunken fishermen returning from the sea, or rather the Oban pubs. My room was next to the toilet door which banged against the bulkhead all night causing me to wake in alarm and wonder where the hell I was. The next problem was the dawn's early light which filtered through the very thin curtains at about four-thirty, printing lace shadows on the ceiling. It was not a good start to the day, but things improved with the bacon and eggs and fried bread which was served up in the galley around seven.

I picked up a newspaper to read with my breakfast. It was Wednesday the eighth of October, 1973. Some kind of war seemed to have broken out in the Middle East. Egyptian and Israeli forces were fighting along the Suez Canal. The Israelis were claiming victory over the Syrians at the Golan Heights. Egypt claimed to have inflicted heavy damage on the Sinai Peninsula. Elsewhere, Len Murray, General Secretary of the TUC, was locking horns with Grocer Heath over Phase Three of the latest pay-bargaining talks.

I spread some toast and marmalade, drained my tea and refilled it with coffee. I could feel a distinct sexual excitement below decks in anticipation of my first helicopter flight.

It all happened very suddenly. For thirty minutes I'd been loafing around the helicopter pad which was right down on the harbourside. Various people came and went, while a few others, like me, loitered palely.

A wiry guy in an orange overall with cropped black hair and Buddy Holly glasses thrust ninety pages of photocopied instructions into my hand with a curt 'Read this, you'll be taking off in five minutes.' I flicked through it wondering where to begin and decided the page that featured a very crude drawing of a head being separated from a running body by a rotor blade would be as good a place as any. Little black teardrop marks signified blood spurting from the severed neck.

'If the helicopter is waiting for you on a low slope,' I read, 'keep your head well down as you run up to enter.' I checked the machine in front of me which looked alarmingly small but was thankfully parked on flat ground by the sea wall. As I'd been reading, the pilot had taken his seat and already the machine was stirring into motion.

Two other men had joined me on the sidelines. One seemed even younger than I was, the other a little older and bearded.

The younger one was as white as chalk. My own attempts at growing a beard were coming along painfully slowly, but in the right light a certain covering of fluff over my lower face was noticeable.

I was angling for a window seat as I had brought my new Rollei camera with me and wanted to try out some aerial photography.

We all bundled in, the white-faced guy in the middle. He was visibly wringing his hands and sweating like a cheese. 'Hi,' I said. 'Are you going to Hyskeir too?'

'Fridge engineer,' he groaned through fixed teeth. 'Repairs,' and I thought he was going to throw up. 'I've never flown before.'

'Neither have I. Should be good fun,' I shouted as the blades spun faster and louder. Then suddenly we were moving, vertically with a little sway to this side and that.

'Oh, Jesus,' my neighbour said, and I noticed his eyes were tight shut.

I was too busy struggling with my aperture to feel nervous, taking eminently forgettable shots of coils of chain and lobster creels. Now we were moving forward, but still remarkably low. Many years later I would fly into the old Hong Kong airport in a 747 and have a similar voyeuristic feeling, watching whole families at their meals and round their television sets as the plane landed between rows of tower blocks. Departing Oban, I could see the upturned faces of fishermen repairing their nets and could almost count the hairs on their chin as we flew above them and out of the harbour. From then onwards it was alternate flashes of sea and land as we skimmed over tiny islands and then open sea. Next to the pilot a life-raft was strapped into the spare seat while the three of us were shoe-horned into the back. My neighbour was still white but at least his eyes were open and fixed hard on his Adidas trainers. We were now flying over Mull, and if you can imagine travelling in a Volkswagen beetle at about two hundred miles an hour a little above the tree line then that is *exactly* what it was like.

At last our pilot turned round to speak to us, although I'd have preferred if he'd kept his eyes on the open sea ahead. We seemed to be flying at a forty-five-degree angle, tilting downwards with a horizon of sea and outer islands slashing across the bubble window.

'I'm Danny,' he introduced himself. All I could see was a helmet and a handlebar moustache. 'More used to flying Sea Kings but these little lawnmowers can be fun. Only one engine though, which is why we have one of these,' and he patted the life-raft reassuringly. 'Not much use if we clip a pylon though,' and I felt that was unnecessary as the fridge engineer mouthed, 'Jesus, Mary, Mother of God. Our Father which art . . .'

'Who's the fridge engineer?' the pilot asked, and the white-faced guy lifted his head as if for execution. 'You'll have the longest run pal,' Danny spoke in the matter-of-fact tones of a hanging judge. 'The other two are aff tae Hyskeir where we'll do the relief and pick up two others. Then it's on to the Flannans to mend their fridge, and once you've done that we have some insulin to drop off at Colonsay on the way back. Fine day for it, though.'

'Ah jist came up frae Glasgow to do the fridge in the Railway Hotel in Oban,' the young engineer was suddenly talkative, shouting to the bearded guy on his right who would be one of my two companions on Hyskeir. 'Then ah get this message on the telephone that ah've to go to a lighthouse and mend a broken freezer cabinet. Ah thought ma boss wis having me on, but no, he says, jen-up it's a lighthouse and there will be a few extra pounds come pay-day. Couldnae say no, like.'

I'm taking masterpieces of the open sea as viewed from above with my camera, the sort of images that would become big in the world of fine art photography twenty years later, signifying the sublime void. All the while I'm listening in to the conversation around me. I hear the other guy introduce himself as Ralph.

'Whit's it like on this lighthouse, then?' the fridge engineer asks the inevitable question.

'I've not been on this one before, but the routine is pretty similar everywhere,' comes the reply. 'I'm training to go full-time so for the past year and a half I've been on different lights all over Scotland.'

And as he speaks – as he shouts – I realise with a strange chill that us two strangers are going to meet up with a third stranger on an uninhabited island in the Outer Hebrides.

'Thank God it's not there,' I said to myself as we flew past a huge lighthouse on a tiny strip of land. We'd passed over several on the flight already, but the one just gone was the most barren looking. Then, to my horror, the helicopter banked and turned in a huge arc, spiralling downwards to the cement landing pad which was decorated with a giant red H that stretched from one side to the other. This was it – Hyskeir.

As we corkscrewed to the ground I could see two men rushing to greet us and a third standing in the shadow of the tower.

There was a flurry of activity. *Our* bags were pulled from the back of the helicopter, *theirs* were thrown in – the rotors kept turning, the noise was painful – and then they were off. The last thing I can remember is the white face of the fridge engineer sandwiched against the dark mass of the two burly keepers off on their leave.

We watched it go, up higher than the tower then, tilting, it sped off towards the Flannan Isles, far beyond Harris. When Ralph and I turned from the now empty sky to face each other the first thing we noticed was that we had been joined by a third party. Three total strangers stood staring at each other, alone on a tiny strip of lava in the North Atlantic.

We shook hands and introduced ourselves, 'Mungo' – 'Ralph' – 'Peter'.

And as we walked across the black lava towards the tallest lighthouse tower I had ever seen, three goats emerged out of the fine sea mist.

The Dalek Invasion of Hyskeir

Mungo Paterson and Ralph Nesbitt were to be my companions for the next fortnight. They were the last two lighthouse keepers with whom I would work. A pot of tea had brewed to a rich dark treacle while the change of crew had been taking place. We gathered round the formica kitchen table and eyed each other warily.

Ralph, as I'd noticed on the helicopter, was bearded and he wore a faded green parka. He looked a little like Eric Clapton from the post-Cream days, and his brown hair coiled around his shoulders. I learned later that he'd started and abandoned several university courses – philosophy, geology, marine biology – before taking an ordinary degree in the philosophy of science. A summer job as a student on the lighthouses two years earlier had somehow continued beyond his graduation and he was in the final months of training as a full-time keeper.

I guessed that Ralph was in his mid-to-late twenties, while Mungo Paterson was close to retirement, which meant over three times my twenty years. If he resembled anyone at all it was Captain Mainwaring as played by Arthur Lowe from the recently popular *Dad's Army* television series. This resemblance was exacerbated by his habit of addressing Ralph and I collectively as 'Men'.

'Alright, men,' he began in an accent which I recognised as having a slight twang of Glasgow's Kelvinside about it. 'We have a strange situation here. We don't know each other from Adam. I am PLK Paterson, but I like my men to call me Mungo – no formalities here. Except on Sundays. We are no longer expected to raise the flag on a Sunday and turn out in full uniform. But it's a tradition I like to keep – join me if you will.'

Ralph and I looked at each other as if to say we'd probably find something else to do at that time, although God knows what. From the kitchen window I could see the black lava of the island stretch in front of us like a submarine and disappear into the greyness of the sea and sky. A sundial, like a stunted periscope, rose from the kitchen garden.

'Now, you men have been on enough lights – I've seen your records – to know that the routine is pretty much the same on all lights.' As Mungo addressed us he filled a short black pipe with tobacco, and Ralph and I took this as a signal to light up an Embassy Regal in his case, and to roll a Golden Virginia in my own.

'But let me tell you a little about this island. They tell me that Hyskeir means "goat island" in the Gaelic. I'm not a speaker, but it's something like "Oigh Sker" or "goat skerry". Anyway, you've met the three goats that live here and the smaller one is in fact the mother of the other two. Now, the island itself. As we'll see in a minute when we go outside it is really three short islands joined by two metal bridges.' Sounded like we were about to take off on an allied bombing mission. 'The tower is at the far end of the first and the fog signal, you will be pleased to learn, is at the opposite end of the third island.' Ralph and I listened with interest, nodding occasionally between mouthfuls of tea.

'These are treacherous seas,' Mungo continued. 'Every few years in a high storm the whole island can be submerged below water. This happened last winter and the well from which we draw our domestic water supplies filled with sea water. Bugger all use unless you're a haddock. So every three months when *The Pole Star* brings our provisions she also brings a three-month supply of water. This you will find in the storeroom next door. What it means men is that we flush the toilet as infrequently as possible. We wash sparingly, and bathe only once a week. This brings me to kitchen duties. Usual routine. One man on lunches all week, other meals shared between the three of us. There's very little to do in the mornings here since we painted the tower and the outhouses in the spring. So we won't be over-extending ourselves during the day.' Fine by me, I thought. 'You can read or sleep. I'm a great Scrabble man myself if either of you cares for a game,' and his eyes lit up hopefully. 'Now, let me show you the meals chart,' and we all rose to our feet and went to inspect a laminated grid in the kitchen which appeared to be about the size of a London Underground map.

'OK. I've already told you the supply vessel comes every three months. We have six freezer units out in the back. Here on the chart,' and he waved the stem of his pipe loosely in front of the grid, 'we can see what we will be having for breakfast, lunch and dinner for any given meal between now and Christmas Day.'

'What will the following grid be like?' Ralph wondered out aloud, and I realised he would be based on Hyskeir for some time.

'Oh, pretty much like this one,' Mungo replied. 'Except the dates will change. It's a good system, I introduced it myself. On my last light up in Shetland the men were always in dispute over meals. They could choose what they wanted every week and the supermarket had a boy who rowed it out. One wanted steak three times a week, and the occasional keeper was a damn fool vegetarian. Anyway, with this system – what I call Paterson's Purvey Chart,' and we took this as a cue to laugh nervously, 'we're never at a loss. Pick any day,' he instructed me as if about to do a magic trick, 'any day you like and we'll see what we've got.'

'The thirty-first of October,' I said at random.

'Good man, Hallowe'en. As you get to know the system you'll see I mark special days, like Easter and Burns night. For breakfast, you see, hazelnut yoghurt, hard-boiled eggs, salami and toast. Then for lunch, pumpkin soup, mince and tatties followed by biscuits and cheese. In the evening we'll have roast lamb with turnip, followed by baked apples and ice cream. Sadly we won't have any guisers chapping at our door,' and I involuntarily began to create a short story in my head, based around 'trick or treat' on a lighthouse.

My wandering imagination was reined in by Mungo turning to today's meal.

'Pretty straightforward stuff. I've scheduled it so that I'm on lunches all this week. Peter, you're doing them next week as that will be your last week, and Ralph is on week three. This afternoon, I'll take you through the ropes *vis-à-vis* the light and the fog signal. Pretty standard stuff, none of your paraffin and air pumps. Hyskeir went electric a few years ago, so it's just a flick of the switch and get the reflectors turning.

'You'll be doing the evening meal tonight Peter, let's see what we've got.' He had to strand on tip-toe to bring himself up to even my fairly small height and with the stem of his pipe located the correct day. 'See,' he exclaimed like a proud father, 'here it is. Fish fingers, baked beans and chips. Two slices of buttered bread, all the bread's white by the way, nothing but the best. Then mince pies and custard. Think you can manage that?'

'No problemo,' I said confidently, but thought wistfully of the near-gourmet meals that Finlay Watchorn used to create on Pladda. Those early days of summer seemed so far away. Halcyon times.

I soon slipped into 'the routine' which was cast from the same mould on each lighthouse. Yet my two weeks on Hyskeir could not have been more different from my two weeks on Pladda, or my eight weeks on Ailsa Craig – *two weeks in a submarine, two weeks in space, two weeks in prison, two weeks in Vietnam* . . . I realise it doesn't sound long, but we're talking life-changing experiences here.

There were no basking sharks, as there had been in the warm Clyde waters, and for a long time it appeared that there weren't any ships either. Then on day ten Mungo shouted across from the vegetable patch to Ralph and myself. We were sitting on a chord of black lava playing with the goats. He was pointing excitedly to the horizon, and when I looked closely I could see it – a tiny dark shape. It might have been a small oil tanker or a large fishing vessel, at that distance it was hard to tell. But the three of us gathered beneath our tower and waved at it like our lives depended on it. To this day I still don't know why. I suppose someone might have been looking at us through binoculars. But I think it was more primeval than that. It was the only ship I saw from Hyskeir in my whole time there.

On the first afternoon Mungo, Ralph and I strolled slowly across the two bridges and three islands to visit the foghorn. Once there we had a smoke and then came back.

We were properly introduced to the three goats on this walk. For some reason the goats decreed that we had to walk in single file in a precise sequence of goat – human, goat – human, goat

– human. If you did not proceed in this way, as I quickly learned, you were butted into place by the mother goat. It made conversation interesting, constantly calling over your shoulder and between goats, but it was a habit we soon picked up.

It was on the return journey that Mungo's complexion darkened and he told us how a keeper had drowned here a few years before. Apparently on a stormy night two of them had gone out to look at the foghorn which wasn't blowing properly. They had both been blown off the first bridge by a freak wave.

'Chance throws some pretty cruel dice,' Mungo paused on the bridge, and I noticed we were all gripping the rail in tight fists. The goats were standing patiently to one side. They allowed us to congregate in small clusters when we were not walking. 'The wave that swept them off gave a final twist and threw one of the men back on the rocks. The other drowned. He was a good man. He is missed.'

The Rembrandts I shared with Ralph and Mungo over the next couple of weeks were bizarre ones. Ralph emerged increasingly like some kind of lost soul, half-child, half-genius, perhaps a symbol for his age. Vietnam, Biafra, the nuclear build-up had, through the reversed telescope of youth, erased long-term plans for any kind of future. The question was, how did we want to spend the present and make the most of our remaining time on planet earth? Just as Ralph had swithered between university courses, leaving one to start another, then giving up again, so it had been with his love life.

'I nearly got married once,' he confessed to me at two in the morning. 'All the invitations had been sent out. Couldnae go through with it. God, it was stressful. We'd even booked our honeymoon in Yugoslavia. She went anyway. I drank my way across to Ireland and spent the summer in Dublin. Then I went back to university. Thought marine biology might be the way to go.'

In the flickering light of the coal fire – each lump carefully measured and transported to us in *The Pole Star* – he looked more than ever like Eric Clapton with his long thin legs draped over the chair. 'You've got your art, Peter,' he would say. 'It'll sustain you for a lifetime, and your writing. But I just don't know what I want to do. And I've met this woman, not that I see much of her in this job. She lives in Oban and has a couple of wee bairns. But I'm still not sure about marriage. When I was a wee kid myself I used to read all these *Superman* comics and I was sure by the time I'd grown up we'd have conquered space and be buzzing about from planet to planet, I really did.'

'Same with me,' I replied. 'I thought we'd be able to dematerialise and then reform in the blink of an eye in another galaxy. Like in *Star Trek*. It's why I've never bothered much with cars. I always thought they'd be obsolete, like the horse and carriage, long before I was old enough to sit my test.'

'At the very least,' Ralph picked up the conversation with some enthusiasm, 'at the very least, we'd have those James Bond backpacks and be flying about the city and bodyswerving the traffic jams.'

'Did you know Sean Connery used to be a life model at the art college in Edinburgh?' I rambled on in the sort of way you do when you are trying to keep your eyes open at two in the morning – free associating for all we were worth. But from that night onwards I knew that if I ever wanted to cheer Ralph up and get the sparkle back in his eyes, science fiction was the way to do it. To be precise, *Dr Who*. Anything to do with *Dr Who*. He could have been a *Mastermind* winner if his specialist subject had been the various incarnations of the chronologically itinerant Time Lord, providing his general questions fell within his various abandoned university courses.

'Do you remember the very first episode?' I asked him, but it was a stupid question. Not only could he give me chapter and verse on how Susan Foreman's teachers, Barbara Wright and Ian Chesterton watch from hiding in the junkyard as the Doctor opens the Tardis door for the very first time, but he could tell me all the little details I'd never even known, such as that the great theme music had been composed by an Australian called Ron Grainer. 'He also did the music for *Steptoe and Son*, *Maigret*, and *The Prisoner*,' Ralph dropped in as an aside. 'But the series really took off with the appearance of the Daleks.' Ah, the Daleks. 'They were a once-noble race of scientists and philosophers,' he continued, a strange Kryptonite-like gleam in his eyes. Outside the lighthouse windows, utter darkness. I got up to brew some more tea for us.

'What made them change?' I asked, never having been fully aware of their history.

'There was a nuclear war and the Daleks were the hideously mutated survivors.' He spoke like an over-eager press release.

'Who wrote the series?' I slipped into the *Mastermind* chair.

'Terry Nation,' came the instant reply.

'And what was your favourite *Dr Who* series?'

'The Dalek Invasion of Earth.'

'Who played the doctor in that series?'

'Patrick Troughton.'

'Can you tell me the name of the first series in which he played the Doctor?'

'The Doctor and the Celestial Toymaker.'

'What was the name of the Daleks' home planet?'

'Skara.'

'Correct. 'Returning to the very first episode, what was it called?'

'An Unearthly Child.'

'And what was unusual about the day it was broadcast?'

'It was the day after President Kennedy was assassinated.'

'Correct. At the end of that round Mr Nesbitt you have scored thirty points, and no passes. It's time I went up and checked on the light. *Adios, amigo.*'

'EXTERMINATE!!!' Ralph shouted after me, his arm extended like Peter Sellers's wheelchair-bound Dr Strangelove. You don't *have* to be mad to work in a lighthouse – but it helps.

There were plenty of newspapers and magazines to read on Hyskeir. The only problem was they were months out of date. Apart from the occasional current tabloid that found its way in at the irregular changes of crew we had to make do with a mixed bag of periodicals that came with the supply ship every three months. One rainy afternoon when the sky was as grey as the sea I chose to read a copy of *The Times* from London for no other reason than it had been published on my birthday, the fifth of June. I know this because I cut out a small news story and folded it inside one of my little yellow notebooks where it still fades slowly to this day. It was headed 'Former Vietnam Prisoner Commits Suicide.'

> Captain Edward Brudno, one of the first American prisoners of war to be released by North Vietnam last February, has been found dead in Harrison, a suburb of New York. Police said that he had committed suicide after being in a state of despondency ever since his return . . . The police say it is the first case of its sort among the 566 prisoners of war who have returned to the United States since February.

I still found myself brooding a lot about Vietnam.

* * *

Whenever possible I tried to get Ralph on to the subject of *Dr Who*, or at the very least science fiction. At those times he was positive, clear, and lucid. On any other subject he would prevaricate, dissemble, change his mind and get lost in self-doubt. Especially on the subject of women. He agreed they were 'a good thing' but wasn't sure how they related to his life or what they expected of him. If he'd been able to turn his broodings into lyrics and strum them to even three basic chords, he would have made a fortune. His last degree, the one he finally finished, hadn't helped his mental state either. 'Doubt is terribly important, Peter,' he once told me at six in the morning when all I wanted to do was sleep for eight hours straight. 'Far more important than faith, in terms of *moving things along*.'

I yawned, and tried to look encouraging. God, I was tired. It had been a very long night. I'd meant to go to bed at eight o'clock and get a decent sleep before starting my watch, but had been lured up longer by the television bait of *Callan* starring Edward Woodward and Russell Hunter as 'Lonely'. Great television, great acting.

'Sir Karl Popper uses the analogy of white swans and black swans,' Ralph continued with a missionary glint in his eye. 'He says that one can sight white swans as often as you like but you will never be able to say that "all swans are white". However, a single sighting of a black swan does allow one to say "Not all swans are white".' He sat back triumphantly as I tried to steer things round to the saner waters of *Dr Who*.

'What about goats?' I wondered, thinking about our three island companions. One of them is black-and-white. Ralph gave me a scornful look.

'It's all about falsifying things rather than constantly trying to verify them,' he explained, gradually unknitting his brows and pouring another cup of tea.

A couple of nights earlier he'd taken me up to the rim of the light and given me a practical demonstration of Wittgenstein's views on why the evening star is not the same as the morning star, linguistically speaking.

'Have you ever read any of Ogden Nash's poetry?' I asked him.

'I don't think I've read any poetry since school,' he replied.

'Well, somewhere he wrote something about "Once you really get thinking about thinking, it's worse than drinking".' I added, 'And as we ain't got any booze here, ahm off tae ma pit.'

Nautical Scrabble

Occasionally I would get out the old atlas from the oak book-case in the living quarters just to check where I actually was. You see, as often as not, looking out the window didn't help as there would only be the grey plains of sky and sea. If a heavy mist settled there would be the sound of the fog signal blowing away on the distant stack of lava. But on a clear, sunny day it was awesome.

From the north-east to the south-west we were surrounded by the islands of Canna, Rum, Eigg, Muck, Coll and Tiree, stud-ding the ocean like a necklace made of very individual gems. Rum stood out tall and dark against the blue and gold sea, and from Hyskeir you felt you could reach out and touch it. Then far to the west, a magical visual event occurred. This happens when there is nothing between your line of sight and the horizon, but over the horizon – beyond your vision – there are other islands, the tops of which *do* rise above the curve of the earth. It is a little like a mirage or a heat haze. At the same time as you can see the curve of the sea in full, you can also see the tops of the islands hovering like clouds of rock from beyond the earth's curve. So it was when we looked west on the one or two hot, clear days that I experienced when the sea was as flat as a mirror. Far to our west rose the islands of South Uist, and across the Sound of Burra to the Isle of Barra, to Vatersay, Sandray, Pabbay, and the romantic sounding Mingulay. Still, we could have been the only three humans left on the planet.

Beyond the Outer Hebrides, there wasn't much until you reached a point on the east coast of North America somewhere between Manhattan and Nova Scotia. And it was from out to the west that a friendly voice I thought I'd never hear again called along the air waves. It was a damp Tuesday afternoon and I was doing the mid-day radio checks when I heard the magical words:

'Ericksay calling, Ericksay here. This is Finlay Watchorn with the lunchtime edition of *Desert Island Discs*. I have to report that Raindrops Keep Falling on our Heads but the PLK and the rest of us here are Singing in the Rain. How is it with you, over?'

'Finlay,' I cried, 'it's Peter Hill here. What are you doing away from Pladda?'

'Guid God, it's John Lennon's wee brother. How's that beard of yours coming along? Has the cat licked the fluff off your chin yet?'

'What are you doing here?' I almost shouted. 'It's great to hear you.'

'Och, 84 were just waiting for me to finish building my boat so they could send me somewhere I couldnae use it. It was a real bugger's muddle. First they were going to send me to the Bass Rock, then they changed their mind and I wasn't going anywhere at all. Then last month I got two week's notice to move my family up here. Or rather, they're in the keeper's houses in Oban and I'm stuck out here like a shag on a rock as Aussie Jim would say. And how's yoursel'?'

We cracked on for a while, until we were both called away for our respective lunches. But over my final week on Hyskeir we managed a couple more chats, with Finlay keeping me up to date on the life and times of Duncan, Stretch, The Professor and Ronnie, who was apparently involved in a romantic relationship with a woman back in the Carse o' Gowrie. 'He's planning to retire soon and open a mushroom farm with his good lady. She's no' got very good eyesight on account of having spent all her life in Perthshire. God it's a dark, dank place is Perthshire. Always avoid it if you have the choice. Their mushroom farm should do well though and they might be able to grow a few tatties in the sunny month.'

Poetry. Ships in bottles. Amateur botany. Solitary self-abuse. Even golf. We all had our hobbies. I think I've mentioned that Mungo Paterson's hobby was the game of Scrabble. However, he'd refined it far beyond its original rules and now played only 'nautical Scrabble'. He was addicted to it and would play the thirty-minute rule with Ralph or myself during the changes of watch. It took me a bit by surprise the first time he woke me up to start a Rembrandt at two in the morning to find the board all set up and the letters ready to be picked from the lid of the box.

'Now, remember,' he said, pouring us each mugs of tea while I cut a hunk of Wensleydale to go with the cream crackers. 'If you can't find a nautical term you can put back and pick again. You'll get the hang of it, a university student like yourself. I missed my chance at *academe* because of friend Hitler,' and he nodded in the general direction of Germany. 'Did my bit for intelligence though,' tapping the side of his nose and winking.

I stared hard at my seven letters and within the three-minute limit that Mungo imposed with the lighthouse egg timer, came up with OAR.

'Not bad for a novice,' he observed, immediately putting down

BOAT running vertically through my OAR. 'Now remember, proper names *are* allowed if they have a nautical connection. NOAH would be permitted, or JONAH for that matter.'

I laboured hard and got JIB which ran horizontally into the B of BOAT. This could be fun, I thought, quickly wakening up. Mungo turned in all his letters but he then went on to get YACHT running into the T of BOAT.

'Do you play any other games?' I asked, trying to place KNOT.

'This is my favourite. Keeps you awake. At my age I find it increasingly hard to stay awake on the later watches. This gets the cogs turning,' and he joined TORPEDO on to my rather pathetic TAR. 'Here's a good one,' he said, putting down PIRATE.

'How about ISHMAEL? Can I have ISHMAEL?'

'ISHMAEL?' he muttered.

'Yes, as in "Call me ISHMAEL", you know the *Moby Dick* story.'

'I'll have to bow to your university education there.' Mungo generously let me have it. It was the highest score I ever made. But I could already see him moving SWAIN across the board and articulating it on to BOAT.

Mungo beat me every time, although I improved over the following two weeks and lost by less each time.

'I was on one light, up in Orkney, where Monopoly was all the rage,' he told me a few nights later. 'But it takes too long and a single game would stretch over several watches. The street names brought back wartime memories though. Leicester Square, Euston Station, Mayfair and Park Lane – not that I saw much of that end of town, although I did take afternoon tea once at the Ritz.' And again he tapped the side of his nose as if there might have been more to it than the quenching of thirst and a nibble on a dry biscuit.

'What about chess?'

'A lot of keepers play chess. Trouble is you need two to play, although I know some who do it by post, or even on the short-wave radio. Lachlan Fairbairn was a great chess player. Have you heard of Lachlan?' And I said, of course, yes I had.

'I was on Chicken Rock with him for some years. And you know I never beat him once. They say he was close to being a Grand Master. He had a difficult war . . .' and Mungo's voice trailed off as he turned in his seven letters for new ones and immediately added SUB to the MARINE that was already there, earning triple points in the process.

'Great linguist too. They say that's what helped get him out of France. Of course by then he was a broken man.'

After intense scrutiny I found DIVE which left the way open for Mungo's VIKING.

'But Lachlan was in the war right from the start. At the outbreak he was working as an engineer on *The Royal Oak* which was sunk by a German U-Boat up in Scapa Flow. He'd have gone down with it too, if he'd been in the engine rooms where he was supposed to be. But one of the officers had been complaining that he couldn't find anyone with whom he could play a decent game of chess. "They say that no one plays a better game than one of our engineers," the Captain remarked and within the hour Lachlan was facing the officer across a small card table on the upper deck. Rumour has it that even in those days he was stark-naked beneath his great coat, but that's rumour for you. Stories tend to grow in the telling – especially on lighthouses.'

'And what happened?' My knowledge of the Second World War was as patchy as it was of the Crusades. I put down SAIL while Mungo reminisced.

'It was the twelfth of October,' he began. 'Two of the lighthouses were switched on at the Pentland Skerries and Roseness, to help our fleet re-group. I was based in Orkney at the time, but not on either of those lights. I wasn't much older than you I suppose, and I had yet to leave for the war. It was the next night that it happened,' and he idly placed MERMAID between two sets of triple points. 'A German U47 submarine crept through the sound where over fifty British ships were anchored. Gunther Prien was captain. He had his eye on the biggest fish, *The Royal Oak* which was way out to the west of the sound beside the old sea-plane carrier *Pegasus*.'

The fire crackled as Mungo threw some more coal on to the tiny pyre and replaced the coal scuttle with a thud. 'It was the third torpedo that really did her in, and she went down in less than fifteen minutes. Lachlan often said to me that there but for the game of chess his grave would have been also.'

I placed RAFT through the A of MERMAID. 'And do you know,' Mungo continued, 'even Winston Churchill himself described the Huns' night of stealth as "a magnificent feat of arms". But war was different then. I don't think you'd get your President Nixon describing an incursion by Ho Chi Minh as "a magnificent feat of arms". Do you? But perhaps war needs to have all glory stripped from it to see it for the evil waste it is.' And with that he more or less won the game, right on the half hour, with TITANIC.

Hitchcock Revisited

My last night on Hyskeir was like a nightmare scripted by Marcel Duchamp, filmed by Alfred Hitchcock and with sets designed by any one of a dozen contemporary conceptual artists. Things had already got bad long before I was woken for my final Rembrandt which would run from two until six in the morning. It wasn't even supposed to be my last night. That should have been twenty-four hours earlier, and by then I should have been safely back on the mainland with a curry and a pint inside me. The day of my official leave-taking had dawned clear and sunny – no danger of fog delaying my departure. The problem was, the lighthouse helicopter was not even in Oban but over on the east coast in Inverness – swathed in the mist and mellow fruitfulness of a Highland autumn.

By midday we received a radio message saying no further attempt would be made that day. 'Cheer up,' Mungo said to me as we cleared away the lunch dishes. 'You'll get ashore tomorrow. Why don't the three of us have a wee game of scrabble?'

'I wouldn't mind a cigarette,' Ralph said. 'I was expecting a couple of cartons of Embassy Regal on the chopper.'

'Me too,' said Mungo, frowning into his packet of No.6. 'Now you come to mention it I've only got six left myself,' and he handed one to Ralph. 'How about you Peter?'

'I've got enough for a couple of roll-ups,' I said, suddenly realising the seriousness of the situation.

No one felt much like scrabble after that. One of the reasons our cigarette stocks were so low was because we had been smoking more than usual the past fortnight as we locked horns in concentration and a fog of smoke over the scrabble board.

We each smoked half a cigarette and nipped the burning tip into the hearth.

'Make them last, men,' Mungo declared. 'We've a long night ahead of us.'

For the rest of the day and into the evening we kept our own counsel and measured our poison with the precision of a morphine nurse. I spent a lot of time sitting on a chord of black lava beside the fog signal, staring across to Rum. Mungo started digging in the vegetable garden and in the light-headedness of nicotine withdrawal I had the surreal suspicion he was digging two graves. Where was Ralph, I wondered anxiously? Then I saw him feeding our scraps from the lunch table to the goats.

After the evening meal, which had been eaten in grumpy silence, we were down to one cigarette each. But was anyone hoarding any? That was the unspoken suspicion.

'I'm going to smoke a third of mine now, and I suggest we all do the same,' Mungo advised. *Coronation Street* was on at the usual time but the Rover's Return was so full of smokers that we switched across to *Barlow at Large*.

Ralph and Mungo looked as miserable as me. Dying for a cigarette. It wasn't just a mental thing, you suffered through every pore in your skin as if they were a million tiny mouths all screaming for nicotine.

'I think I'll go to my bed. Two o'clock watch tonight,' I said.

'See you, pal,' from Ralph.

'See you.'

I woke up before the bell. There was this incredible tapping which in my nightmare had been the sound of me in my coffin in the vegetable patch trying to break out. I had an almost immediate craving for a cigarette, for ten cigarettes, for a field of tobacco pl . . . But the tapping continued, it hadn't just been in my dreams. Something was tapping and scratching at the window. I pulled on my clothes in the dark and raced through to the kitchen. Mungo was surprised to see me as it was a good twenty minutes before I was due to start my last watch.

He had the black plastic rubbish bag out on the kitchen table looking for cigarette ends. The lights were off and he was using a torch. I felt like I had woken up in a Samuel Beckett play.

'Have you got any cigarette papers, Peter? I've got enough here for two smokes, maybe three. Keep one for Ralph . . .' his voice trailed off. How the mighty had fallen.

'What's with the tapping?' I asked.

'Turn the light on and you'll see,' Mungo commanded.

I flicked the switch. At first the windows seemed their usual two in the morning black. Then I saw the eyes, hundreds of them and more arriving each second, accompanied by bumps and thuds.

'It's the birds,' Mungo explained. 'They've arrived.'

I'd never seen anything like it. Feathers and beaks and eyes and claws seemed to carpet the window with a double layer of darkness.

I must have looked white.

'Turn off the light,' Mungo's voice sounded strained, and I noticed his fingers were nicotine stained up to the second knuckles. I'd never noticed that before. His must be a great addiction, I thought.

'What's happening?' I asked. I didn't understand.

'You should take a look outside.'

He came with me. 'Don't let any of them in,' he warned, and we both ducked outside quickly. I remember being hit by the sudden cold. Then I looked upwards. There were thousands and thousands of birds, circling in the beam of the turning light. Even from the ground I could tell they were of different sizes, different types, specks of wren and blobs of thrush and red-wing. But they glided round so gracefully, as if on a carousel, the full moon appearing like speckled stars between their overlapping wings. I've never seen anything quite like it before or since. For a moment I even stopped thinking about cigarettes. Round and round they went, following the beams of light. But there were thousands more. Mungo tapped me on the shoulder and pointed to the ground. For as far as I could see, and in the shadow of the tower, the earth seemed to be bubbling with a frothy carpet of feathers. 'There could be half a million, I don't know . . .' Mungo gestured with both arms. 'It happens twice a year. The land birds from Scandinavia heading south to Africa for the winter. Then they come back in the spring. Regular as the clockwork that drives our beacon.'

He ushered me indoors and gave me one of the three cigarettes he'd rolled and lit one himself. 'Sea birds generally stay away from lighthouses. But land birds navigate their way south from lighthouse to lighthouse. I've often wondered how they used to do it, before lighthouses. The stars I suppose – magnetic fields,' he trailed off mystically. I sat up all night once, watching them. They seem to fly in on the beam and circle for maybe half an hour, slowly coming down till they settle on the ground. As they descend their place is taken by others, so there is a constant stream coming in all night. You'll find a few up in the light chamber. They get in through the roof of the light, where the paraffin vapour used to escape before Hyskeir went electric.

'It's like being in a coffee percolator full of birds up there. I just wind the light and get out quick. Spend your watch in the kitchen, that's my advice,' and he nipped his roll-up in two. 'Good luck, I'm going to my bed. I'll put Ralph's cigarette by his bed, stop either of us smoking it.' And with that he was gone. I was left feeling like the only actor in a nautical remake of *The Birds*.

I turned off the kitchen light and climbed the tower for the first winding of my watch. It was a very tall tower and there were at least a dozen black windows cut into its walls. As I climbed upwards, every window was alive with birds and the whole tower filled with the sound of their beaks tapping against the glass. Inside the chamber there were at least thirty flapping wildly about, some with broken legs, some with broken wings. In the intense beam of the light above me their winged shadows stretched to thirty feet in length then contracted to the size of a penny. I shielded my face with my left arm and wound the light as quickly as I could with my right. Occasionally I felt a claw digging through my pullover as the weight seemed to take all eternity to rise up. Feathers brushed my hair and cheeks. I paused long enough to notice that outside the light on the various rails that enclosed the glass dome, hundreds of birds sat shoulder to shoulder, looking inwards, directing their gaze, it seemed, at me. Me with only half a cigarette left and four hours ahead. I raced down the stairs three at a time and slumped into an armchair. It was going to be a long, trying night.

The next morning was like the calm after a battle. Most of the birds had gone, but one in a thousand had flown straight into the light like a moth to fire and broken their necks on the lighthouse glass. I'd seen it happen many times during the night, and heard it too. All of the outhouses around the tower had flat roofs, and when we removed the dead ones from around the light, and caught and released those still alive and frightened in the chamber, we looked down from the tower and saw that the flat roofs were carpeted with dead birds. It was one of the saddest sights I'd ever seen, yet strangely it looked like a surreal art work. We picked them up like plump leaves and threw them into the cold sea. Inverness had called to say the helicopter was on its way. It was picking up at two other lights and would be at Hyskeir by noon. My bags were packed and I'd eaten my last lighthouse breakfast. We had been kept busy with the birds and our mass burial at sea. But now we all just longed silently, inwardly, for a cigarette. I'd noticed that Mungo had a couple of scrabble pieces in his right hand which he clicked against each other obsessively.

It had been one of the best summers of my life, I reflected, staring across a slate-grey sea to the distant islands that had become like staunch friends. But where now? I thought back to Pladda and Ailsa Craig. I even had my first photographs taken with my new pocket-sized Rollei camera with the collapsible lens, developed and printed whilst on shore leave. Some of the shots of The Craig would make you think it was the Mediterranean and not the west coast of Scotland. There was a golden hue to the cliff face, speckled with the white of nesting gannets and framed by the oh-so-blue sky. Could I live like this forever, I wondered? A month on, a month off, two weeks holiday a year. Free house and a travel allowance. But I felt there were other adventures up ahead. Maybe in a few years time I'd return to keeping the light. I'd now completed eighty thousand words of my novel – one thousand words slowly handwritten on every watch – and was excited to get it typed up. I'd use part of my money from Hyskeir to buy a typewriter, and then ever so slowly, one finger at a time, I would teach myself to type. I'd put enough in my post office account to live on for at least six months. And then what? Back to art school, or on to other adventures. Back to the lighthouses? No, in some ways my short spell keeping the lights would stay fresh, I felt, if they were not allowed to become repetitious and everyday.

Some of the great men I'd worked with had been merchant seamen at one time or another and I'd quizzed them about cheap and adventurous ways to get to South America. To a man they'd all recommended The Blue Star Line. Apparently I could work my passage or, for far less than a ticket on an ocean liner, I could pay to go as a passenger and live with the crew. And why South America? It seemed exotic to me, as working on the lighthouses had before I landed that job. Authors I'd been reading in my various lighthouse beds – Thor Heyerdal, Allen Ginsberg, Carlos Casteneda – all seemed to point in that direction. Perhaps if the book got published and I made a little money I would set off for Chile or Mexico. If not, then I still remembered what the two photographers on Ailsa Craig had said about their art school in Guildford. Not that I was quite sure yet where Guildford was. Close to London by the sound of it, and that was still an exciting place to be in the early 1970s.

I picked up a small corner of lava that had chipped off one of the black chords of lava that was our home, and put it in my donkey jacket. Two years ago I'd just finished high school. Now, I felt, my real education had begun.

Then I saw it, a tiny dot approaching out of the sun from the direction of Barra. I was going home.

The chopper did a wide loop of the lighthouse and landed bang in the centre of the pad.

I passed Ralph the poem I had transcribed a few hours earlier.

Mungo slapped me on the back and challenged me to a game of scrabble next time we met.

'Maybe "poetical Scrabble",' I shouted above the rotors. 'Or "rock music Scrabble". Chance to win, like.'

My replacement jumped out and I squeezed in with my kit beside two other home-bound keepers. As we took off I could see him pass a carton of cigarettes to Mungo's outstretched arms and a wad of letters from family and friends.

'Oban, here we come!' the pilot shouted over his shoulders. I grinned at the keeper sitting next to me, a big man in a black oil-skin. The returning keeper at the other window was gazing down below at the disappearing dot of Hyskeir.

He turned around once it had vanished into the grey sea, and to my astonishment I was met by the grinning face of Finlay Watchorn topped by his Greek fisherman's hat and looking for all the world like Captain Haddock.

'My shout in the Harbour Bar,' he said. 'Widen the gutters, we're coming home!'

POSTSCRIPT

Ocean Necklace

1999: Twenty-five years later

Imagine looking down on Australia from above. The world's largest island is ringed with an ocean necklace of lighthouses. Stretching from up near Papua New Guinea to down near Antarctica, from Perth, the world's most isolated city, across to Sydney on the eastern seaboard.

My story began on Pladda – a tiny island off the larger island of Arran, itself dwarfed by the island of mainland Britain. Twenty-five years later I am experiencing the same thing but on the other side of the world. Islands, like tiny Russian dolls, found alongside ever-larger ones. Beneath the big island of Australia – about the same size as the USA – is the magical island state of Tasmania, roughly the size of Scotland. And alongside the southern end of Tasmania is Bruny Island. That's where I am, looking up to a wonderful lighthouse under the perfect blue skies and the same warm sun that greeted me on my first day on Pladda.

Since I was a keeper, lighthouses have gradually – then ever more swiftly – been automated. First the fog signals, then the beacons themselves, were automated – and the humans were needed no more. Some have become up-market bed-and-breakfast establishments. Those with helicopter landing pads make good corporate retreats. Others sit empty, their beams turning like the eyes of giant robots scanning the oceans.

Over the past few months country after country has announced that their final manned lighthouses have been automated – Scotland, Australia, France, Japan, New Zealand, Canada. But these reports are not always true. Andy and Beth, the Bruny Island keepers, are still here, but are now employed by Parks and Wildlife. The light can look after itself, but they still check the weather and send reports to the mainland twice a day.

The other lighthouse keepers' cottage was sitting empty until recently. Now it is inhabited by two artists – Joyce Hinterding and David Haines from Sydney. They are what is known as 'sound artists'. They have the sort of equipment with them that scared the hell out of me on Pladda. Knobs, dials, and small black screens that occasionally flutter with static. I am visiting Bruny with a group of forty or so art gallery directors from all over Australia who are having their annual conference in Hobart. Joyce and David explain to us that they are pulling signals down from polar orbiting satellites and transforming the radio waves into images. They say they can tell the Russian ones from the Americans and know when they are about to appear overhead.

After the demonstration we drift out across the mossy grass and over the white rocky road to where tables have been set up with wine and champagne and plates of the most exquisite Tasmanian oysters. Behind us is the coach that brought us all down. In front, the lighthouse, and beside me Andy the keeper.

We talk, we enthuse, we get passionate together about light-houses, and it is not long before we drift away from the crowd and climb the stairs together. We step out on to the rim of the light. Far below the sea hammers the rocks.

We compare notes. How many keepers were on your lights? How long did you work without a break? What were the meals like? Did they move you from light to light? Were there many mad bastards? 'Someone needs to tell our story,' Andy says, half in hope, half in anger. 'Mate, once we die that's it. No one will know what it was like. I keep in touch with guys in Adelaide and Darwin and Rottnest. Someone needs to write down their stories. Look down there,' and he pointed to the rocks below. 'A convict ship from England went down there. Everyone got ashore, and their powder was dry too. The guards shot all the prisoners. What happened to the aborigines in Tassie was worse of course . . .'

The stories kept tumbling out. And it was only then that I fully realised that the profession of lighthouse keeper was perhaps the only one that paid you to tell stories. Stories to keep your colleagues awake at night so they could turn the light and start a new watch. I wanted to collect those stories like a bee keeper collects honey. Perhaps it was time to travel around the world's biggest island and write it all down. Perhaps it was time to visit the jewels of this great ocean necklace.